The Elegant
Japanese
House

The Elegant Japanese House

Traditional Sukiya Architecture

text *by* Teiji Itoh

photographs by Yukio Futagawa

WEATHERHILL / TANKOSHA
New York • Tokyo • Kyoto

This book was originally published in Japanese in 1967
by Tankosha, Kyoto, under the title *Sukiya*. The present
text has been translated and, in consultation with the
author, adapted for Western readers by the staff of John
Weatherhill, Inc., under the editorship of Ralph Friedrich.

The book design is based upon that of the original
edition, whose visual concept and presentation was by
Ikko Tanaka, and uses the same photograph and diagram
pages.

Title-page decoration: the word *sukiya* in calligraphy by
Yukihiko Yasuda, member of the Japanese Academy of
Arts and a leading Japanese-style painter.

First edition, 1969
Second printing, 1978

*Jointly published by John Weatherhill, Inc., of New York and
Tokyo, with editorial offices at 7-6-13 Roppongi, Minato-ku,
Tokyo 106; and Tankosha, Kyoto. Copyright © 1969 by
Tankosha; all rights reserved. Printed in Japan.*

LCC No. 68-26952
ISBN 0-8348-1500-1

Table of Contents

Guide to Illustrations

Author's Foreword

Since this book does not begin with a lengthy explanatory introduction and statement of purpose but, instead, invites the reader to make his own unobstructed approach to the *sukiya* style, it may be well here to make a few prefatory remarks.

In an earlier book, *The Essential Japanese House: Craftsmanship, Function, and Style in Town and Country* (1967), we treated at length the *minka* or folk-house style; here we turn to the other side of the coin, the elegant sukiya style, and the two books together thus form a unified approach to the two principal traditional styles surviving in Japanese domestic architecture today. As for the present book, if it has any other reason besides the main one of revealing the essential values of the sukiya style, it is that this style, in its planning methods, its sensitive use of materials, and its aesthetic consciousness, has had a great influence on modern Japanese architecture and has extended this influence to Western architecture as well. As we shall note, in this respect, the modern architect has much to learn from that most typical of sukiya creations, the Katsura villa, even though it was built as long ago as the seventeenth century. In a very real sense, then, the values of the sukiya style are still very much alive and valid today.

In his progress through the three main parts of the book, the reader will be invited to look first at a modern structure in sukiya style, the Kitamura residence in Kyoto, and thereby to arrive at a basic understanding of the style. In the second part he will be taken on a journey of exploration into the history of the style and will be provided with views of its essential characteristics. In the third part he will have the opportunity to observe in detail its most typical features and their role in creating the total atmosphere of the sukiya-style building. And throughout, since this book concerns itself as much with function as with design and craftsmanship, attention is given to the social environment in which the sukiya style evolved, as well as to its applicability in the rapidly changing world of today.

The reader will note the conspicuous absence of modern sukiya-style residences, except for that of Mr. Kitamura. I had hoped to include more of them, but to my great regret I discovered that very few of them are appropriately maintained.

There has been no effort at chronological arrangement of the illustrations, which would have been contrary to the concept and intended rhythm of the book—and would, in any case, have been uninspiring. For similar reasons no effort has been made, except in Part 1, to group the illustrations according to the structures they portray. Those of the Katsura villa, for example, appear at various places throughout the book. None of this, however, need inconvenience the reader, since the text carries pertinent cross references to both photographs and plans, and the index lists all the illustrations for each structure presented.

The brief captions that accompany the illustrations are supplemented by the Commentaries on the Photographs at the back of the book, where the photographs are described in some detail. It should be noted that the numbers of the commentaries are those of the pages on which the photographs appear.

The names of all modern (post-1868) Japanese in the book are given in Western style (surname last)—for example, Isoya Yoshida. Those of premodern Japanese appear in Japanese style (surname first)—for example, Toyotomi Hideyoshi.

TEIJI ITOH

The Elegant
Japanese
House

木目

PART ONE

The Sukiya Style Exemplified: Kitamura Residence, Kyoto

To define the sukiya style of Japanese architecture as an evolution from the ceremonial teahouse of the feudal period is to be both conventional and concise but not to be particularly enlightening or even altogether accurate. As we shall presently see, the matter is a good deal more complicated than this. For the time being, then, let us say that the sukiya style is one of the two chief traditional styles surviving in Japanese residential architecture today (the other being the *minka* or folk-house style), that it represents a refinement of elements and techniques borrowed mainly from the earlier teahouse and from the minka as well, and that it is characterized by a freedom of planning and construction and an individuality of treatment that set it apart from all other styles. Admittedly, such a definition is no model of conciseness, but at least it will serve as a beginning, until we reach Part 2, with its expansion of this definition.

Rather than extend these remarks into a lengthy prologue in words, it has seemed better here to demonstrate the essential characteristics of the sukiya style at once with an outstanding example in pictures. For this reason the entire first part of the book is given to the residence of Kinjiro Kitamura in Kyoto, and the photographs and plans that make up this part are intended to lead the reader into the subject without setting up the obstacle of a long-winded and no doubt unprofitable preliminary discussion. Later sections of the book will clarify, both in words and in pictures, the origin and development of the sukiya style, so that, at the end, the reader will arrive at an understanding of its essence.

Kinjiro Kitamura comes of an old family of wealthy dealers in fine building woods, with large tracts of forest land in the mountainous Yoshino region, south of Nara, which produces some of Japan's most prized woods. By family inheritance, training, and personal preference, he is vitally interested in Japanese materials and building methods, a fact which explains the perfection of his own residence.

The Kitamura residence is located beside the Kamo River in the section of Kyoto called Kamikyo-ku. The river itself is hidden from the grounds by a dike and a hedge and thus cannot be considered as "borrowed scenery"—the distant views often incorporated into Japanese garden and landscape settings as part of the picture. Instead, the setting here borrows a vista of the mountain Nyoigatake, which shows itself in a variety of moods: sometimes a silhouette in green, sometimes draped with mist, sometimes vanishing in rain. Every year, on the evening of August 16, at the height of one of Kyoto's famous festivals, a huge bonfire in the shape of the Japanese character for "great" (大) is lighted on the flank of the mountain, and on that evening the view of Nyoigatake from the Kitamura residence is dramatic indeed.

The whole compound covers an area of about 2,330 square yards or somewhat less than one-half acre—in traditional Japanese measurement, 590 *tsubo*. In earlier times the land was part of the estate of two noblemen in succession: first, Prince Kajii and then Baron Fujita. In 1936, when the estate was broken up for sale in lots, Mr. Kitamura purchased part of it as a site for a new residence, and in 1944, after five years of work made particularly difficult by wartime conditions, construction was completed under the supervision of a master carpenter who happens to bear the same surname, Sutejiro Kitamura. The residence then consisted of the main gate, the living quarters, a tea-ceremony house, a storehouse, a separate *shoin*—that is, a structure designed for use as a study or for the entertainment of guests—and the surrounding garden. All of the sukiya-style buildings of the residence shown in this book are the original ones.

At the end of the Pacific War the residence was requisitioned for use by the occupation forces, and the buildings thereby suffered a certain amount of damage. In 1963 the living quarters and the storehouse were remodeled according to a design by the eminent architect Isoya Yoshida. These new structures are reinforced concrete, although the rooms of the living quarters are basically in the sukiya style. The garden designer was Etsushu Sano.

The Kitamura mansion goes by the name of Shikunshi-en, which may be translated as "Dwelling of the Four Gentlemen." The "four gentlemen" are the four noble plants of traditional Chinese and Japanese art and literature—the chrysanthemum, the bamboo, the plum, and the orchid—and the allusion is a pertinent one, since it implies a certain elegance of taste and style. Interestingly enough, the Japanese names of the "four gentlemen" also involve a pun on the owner's name.

The teahouse also has a name of its own, equally allusive. It is called Chinchiriren, which is both the nickname of the master of the house and a refrain from Japanese classical music, a hobby of Mr. Kitamura's. Again, the name carries the implication that Mr. Kitamura is not as skillful as his teacher in the performance of such music—an indication not only that he is adept at classical allusions but that he has a sense of humor as well. Perhaps the modest size of the tearoom itself has something to do with this, for it is quite small, covering an area of only about 8.6 square yards (a little over 2 tsubo in Japanese measurement). It takes the form known as *sanjo-daime-nakaita*: 3 *tatami* (floor mats) of regular size, one of the smaller *daime* size, and an uncovered and unpainted

◀ Flooring of unpainted wood

section of wooden flooring *(nakaita)*. As we shall presently see, the tearoom in a sukiya-style building symbolizes the origin of the sukiya style itself and thus, regardless of its size, is an element of prime importance.

A house in sukiya style, even though it has been beautifully constructed, does not achieve its true being through perfection of form and design alone. Depending upon how the inhabitants use and control the space, the atmosphere may be attractive and refined or disorderly and cheap-looking. If those who occupy the house fail to reflect the elegance of the environment in their own daily life, the house will lose its original beauty. They may, for example, own all sorts of valuable art objects suitable for display in the tokonoma (decorative alcove), but they must not display more than one piece at a time. They may love flowers, but unless they can appreciate a simple arrangement of common flowers and view it as a luxury, they will violate the aesthetics of space and form in the sukiya-style house. No matter how expensive and wonderful imported art objects and Western flowers may be, they have no place in the sukiya environment, for they are completely alien to it. The canons of sukiya taste are perhaps rigid, but that they are elegant cannot be denied.

The Kitamura residence is by no means the only sukiya masterpiece that comes to us from the hands of outstanding designers and craftsmen, but it is one of the few examples in which the spirit of the master craftsmen and the admirable personality of the owner are brought together in perfect harmony to preserve the true flavor of the traditional sukiya style. And for this reason it serves as an excellent definition of the style itself.

表門の正面

北村家の屋敷断面図と平面図
Plan of Kitamura Residence, Kyoto

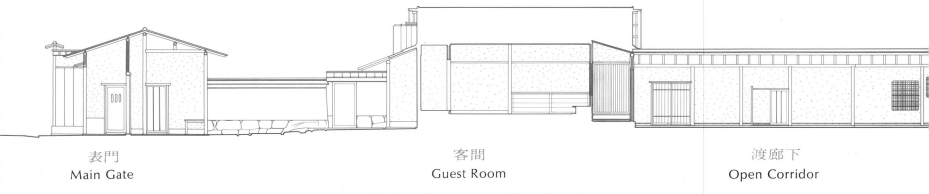

表門
Main Gate

客間
Guest Room

渡廊下
Open Corridor

The sukiya-style portions of the residence appear in black at the bottom of the plan; those built of reinforced concrete are shown in white at the top.

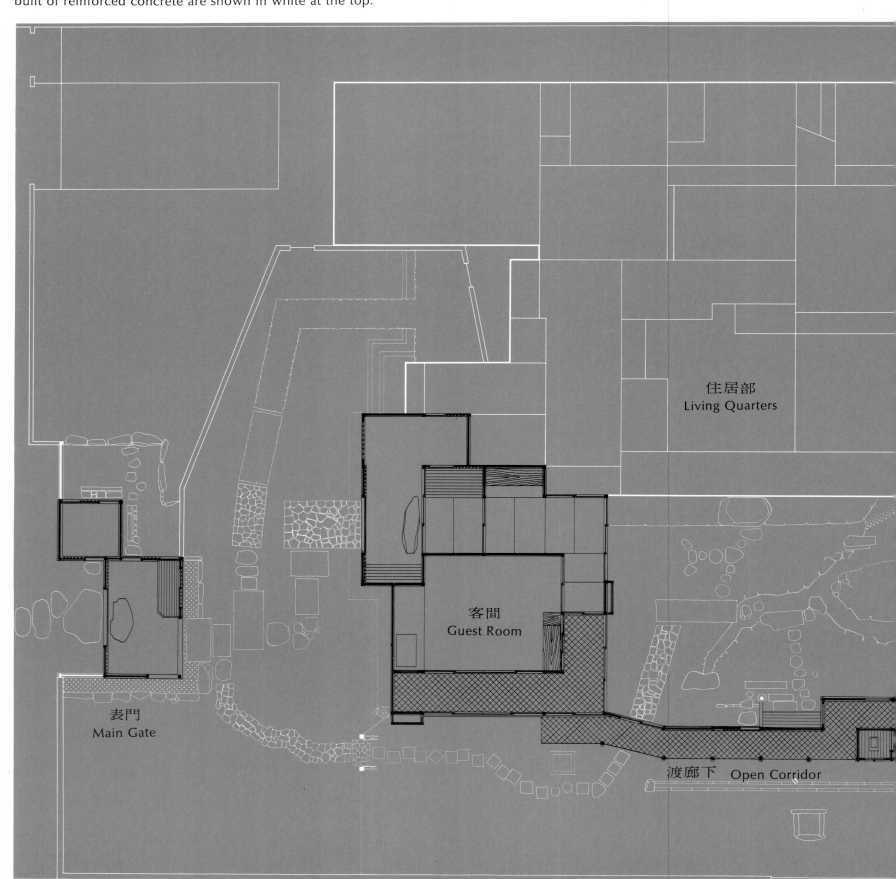

住居部
Living Quarters

表門
Main Gate

客間
Guest Room

渡廊下 Open Corridor

◀ Main gate, Kitamura residence, Kyoto

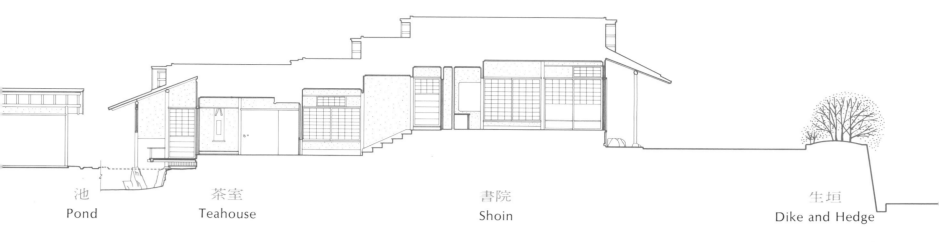

池
Pond

茶室
Teahouse

書院
Shoin

生垣
Dike and Hedge

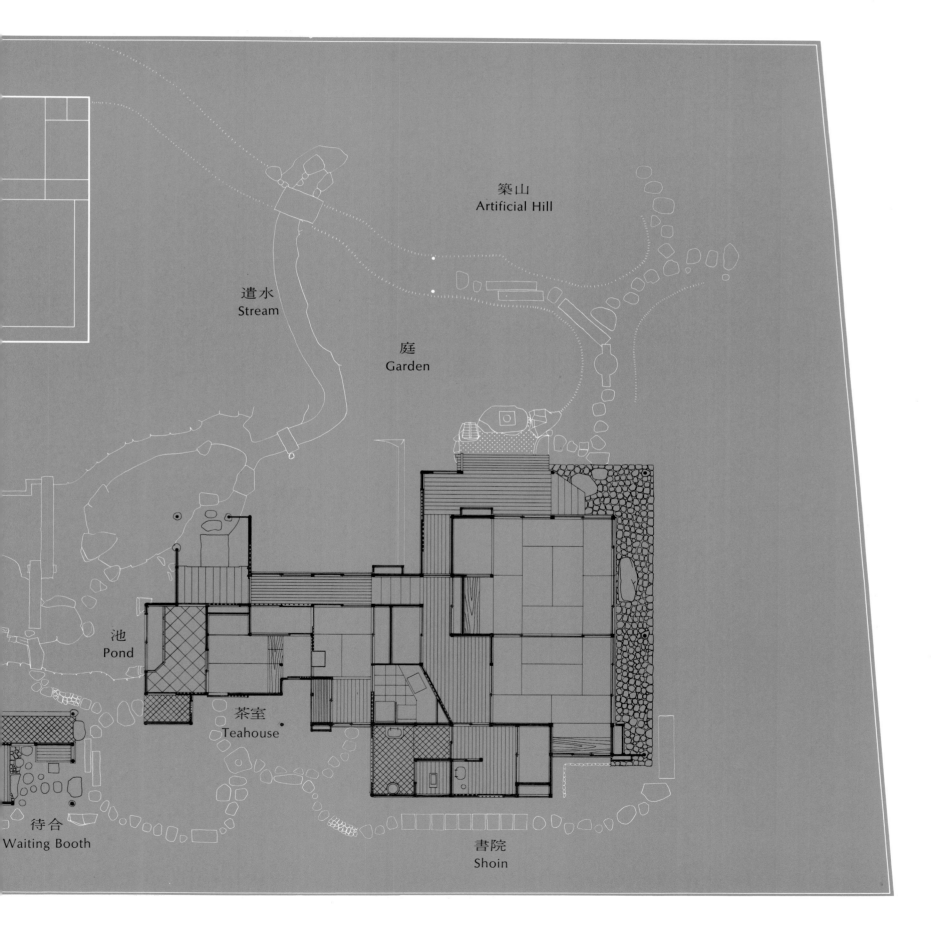

築山
Artificial Hill

遣水
Stream

庭
Garden

池
Pond

茶室
Teahouse

待合
Waiting Booth

書院
Shoin

表門から庭門をみる

◀ View from inside main gate, Kitamura residence, Kyoto

Main entrance, Kitamura residence, Kyoto

住宅の玄関

◀ Two views of open corridor from guest room to teahouse, Kitamura residence, Kyoto

Machiai (waiting booth), Kitamura residence, Kyoto

Steppingstone path, Kitamura residence, Kyoto　　　左—待合　　右—露地の手水鉢

◀ Pond and teahouse veranda, Kitamura residence, Kyoto

Teahouse veranda, Kitamura residence, Kyoto

Interior of tearoom, Kitamura residence, Kyoto　　左—茶室の縁　　右—茶室の内部

Teahouse, Kitamura residence, Kyoto

茶室の西面

Corridor from teahouse to
shoin (view toward shoin),
Kitamura residence, Kyoto

左—茶室から書院への廊下　右—書院から茶室への廊下

Corridor from teahouse
to shoin (view toward
teahouse), Kitamura
residence, Kyoto

Veranda of shoin, Kitamura residence, Kyoto 書院の縁

Detail of stonework, Kitamura residence, Kyoto

Stone-paved passageway under eaves of shoin, Kitamura residence, Kyoto　　左—書院の沓脱石　　右—書院の庇

書院の雪見障子

◀ Interior of shoin, Kitamura residence, Kyoto

Bamboo blinds in shoin, Kitamura residence, Kyoto

Corridor window of shoin, Kitamura residence, Kyoto　　左—書院の簾　　右—書院廊下の花頭窓

Guest room of shoin, Kitamura residence, Kyoto   書院の床間と違棚

北村邸の吹抜平面透視図

Plan of Kitamura Residence, Kyoto

Only the sukiya-style buildings of the residence are shown.

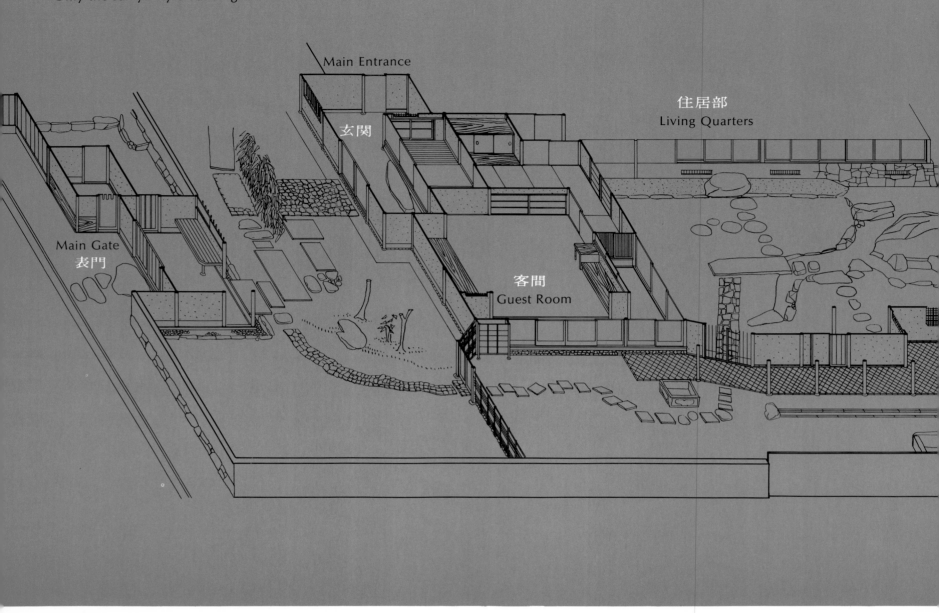

Main Entrance
玄関
住居部
Living Quarters
Main Gate
表門
客間
Guest Room

西側軒の断面詳細図

Detailed Section of Teahouse Eaves (West Side)

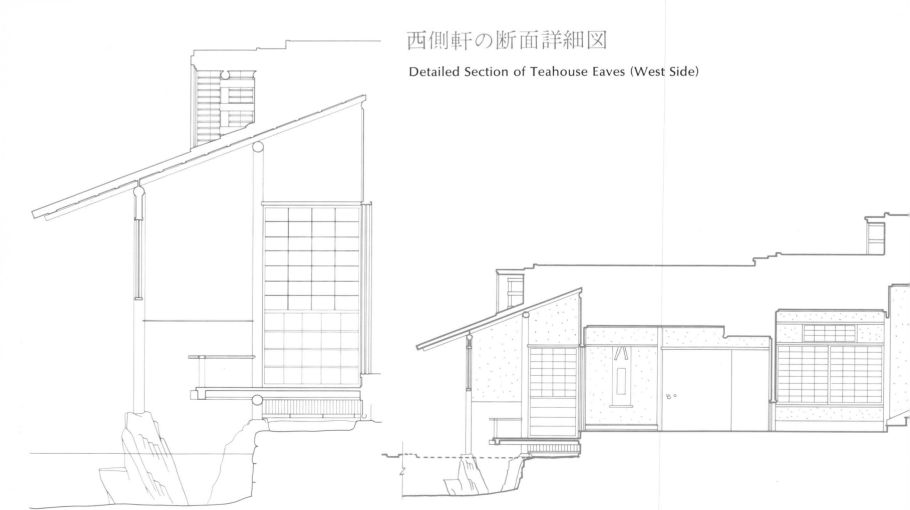

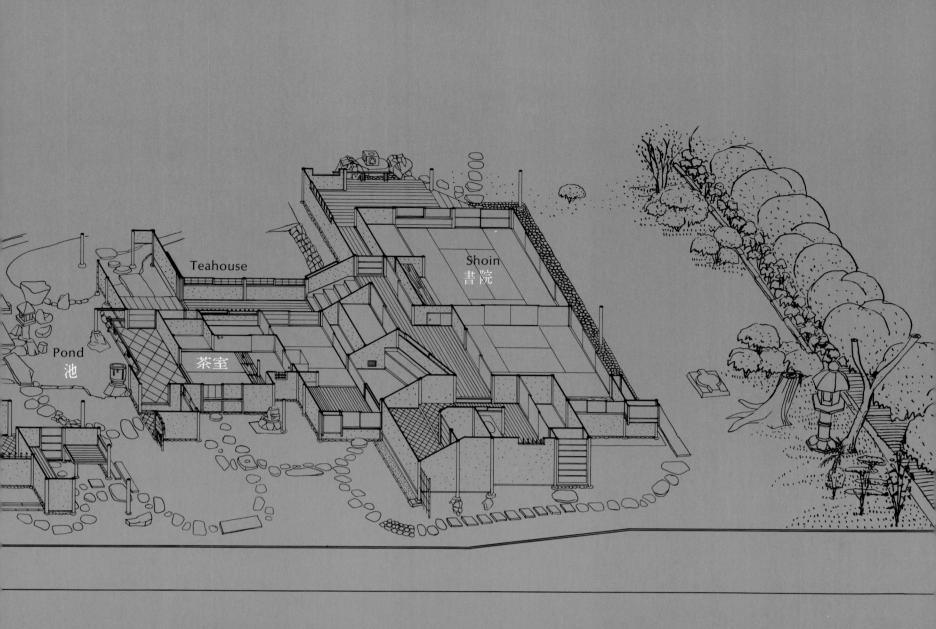

Pond
池

Teahouse

茶室

Shoin
書院

茶室および書院の東西断面図

East-West Section of Teahouse and Shoin

東側軒の断面詳細図

Detailed Section of Shoin Eaves (East Side)

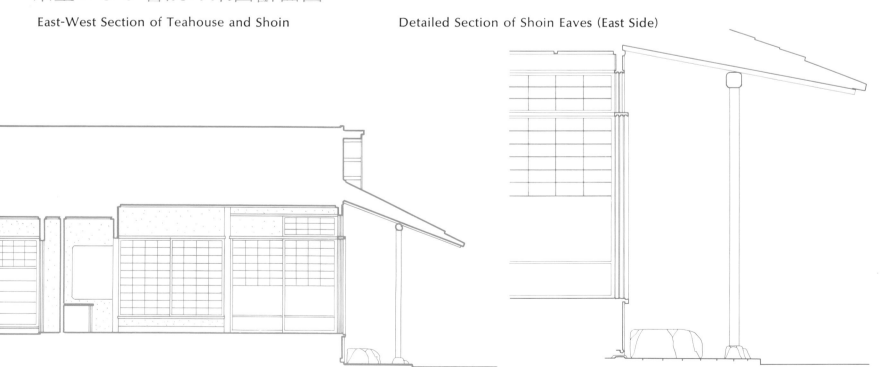

The Realization of the Sukiya Style

In tracing the origin and development of the sukiya style we must begin by distinguishing two meanings of the word "sukiya." In its basic sense it means a teahouse: an independent structure built for performing the tea ceremony. By extension it also means any structure built with the architectural techniques of the teahouse. When one room in a house is used as a *chashitsu* or tea-ceremony room, this room is not called a sukiya but a *kakoi* (literally, "enclosure"), and the house itself may or may not be in the sukiya style. In Japanese the sukiya style is known as *sukiya-zukuri* or *sukiya-fushin,* both expressions having the literal meaning of "sukiya construction." This book deals with both types of the sukiya—the separately built teahouse and the structure built in teahouse style—although it gives more space to the latter. Occasionally, for purposes of clarity, the text makes use of the term "sukiya teahouse," even though this is technically a tautology.

While one might assume that it would be easy to differentiate the two sukiya types because of their relative size, logically expecting the teahouse to be smaller, this is not the case. In fact, the teahouses in the early period of sukiya development (sixteenth and seventeenth centuries) were often rather large, and many of the buildings that copied their style (but not their purpose) were actually smaller. It is therefore not easy to distinguish the two types by exterior appearance alone. When most Japanese speak of the teahouse or tearoom today, they tend to think of a small area of not more than 4.5 mats. As a matter of fact, it is this type that we frequently see pictured in books and magazines. But without a *katte* (kitchenette or pantry) and a *mizuya* (place for washing tea-ceremony utensils) the tea ceremony cannot be performed, and often these adjuncts to the tearoom itself are accompanied by other rooms, such as those for the reception of guests. A building with all these facilities already makes a small house. For example, the Ryokaku-tei (pages 85, 132–33, 148, 192–93), located on the premises of the Ninnaji temple in Kyoto and reputedly once owned by the celebrated artist Ogata Korin (1658–1716), has five rooms and is almost as large as the average dwelling house.

When the sukiya structure serves purely as a setting for the tea ceremony, it may also be called a chashitsu (the word is used interchangeably for "teahouse" and "tearoom"), but it is important to remember that other buildings in the sukiya style are not merely copies or enlargements of the tea-serving area itself. Houses, restaurants, and inns were influenced not only by the techniques used in the limited space in which the tea ceremony was performed but also by the total arrangement of the building, including such adjuncts as the above-mentioned katte and mizuya as well as additional areas such as reception rooms for guests. Thus we would miss the essence of sukiya-style planning if we were to think of the tearoom alone and ignore its combination with other rooms. In a word, it is necessary to pay attention not only to the separate details of architecture in the tearoom but also to the arrangement system of the entire building, to the principles of aesthetic harmony that it displays, and to the quality of the materials that have been used in the construction. All of these elements are most important to an understanding of the sukiya style.

Two main traditional systems of planning survive in Japanese residential architecture today. The first of these is to be seen in the minka, the houses of the common people built in town and country, and dates back to early times. For the sake of convenience we may call it the minka system and briefly define it as planning based on a fixed structural design. The other system, with which we are concerned in this book, is of more recent origin, having appeared in the latter half of the sixteenth century. It is known as the sukiya system, and it differs from the minka system in not being limited by a basic structure of fixed form. In addition to these, of course, the Japanese evolved other architectural styles and systems of planning—for shrines and temples, for court architecture, and for the residences of the aristocracy, to name the principal ones—but it is the minka and the sukiya systems that are of immediate interest here.

Although these two systems of architectural planning present marked contrasts to each other, as will be noted presently, the sukiya system was not created as a repudiation of the minka system. This may sound a bit strange to Western readers, who tend to view new cultural developments in terms of the repudiation of older ones, but it is typical of architectural development in Japan, where varying systems and styles tend to coexist rather than to dominate or supplant one another. In fact, the sukiya system in its early period was considered as a variation of the minka system, and therefore their relation should not be interpreted as that of husband and wife, let us say, but that of father and son—in a word, one of derivation rather than of polar opposites. Nor can we forget that Sen no Rikyu, the man who fathered the sukiya style, was both a prosperous townsman of Sakai and a tea master of remarkable aesthetic perception who did not hesitate to borrow from the minka style in creating a new style of his own. Rikyu will figure prominently in the sections that follow.

1. Origins: Sen no Rikyu and His House at Juraku-dai

Sen no Rikyu (1521–91) was one of the outstanding figures of the Momoyama period (1573–1615), an age that was to become a symbol for splendor in Japanese art and architecture. In 1582 the military dictator Toyotomi Hideyoshi achieved supreme power in Japan, and his taste for luxury and ostentation set the pace for the times. Magnificent buildings were erected one after another, among them Hideyoshi's castle in Osaka; the great temple in Kyoto known as the Hoko-ji, built under Hideyoshi's instructions; and his two Kyoto castles, Juraku-dai and Momoyama-jo, the latter of which gave its name to the period. In relation to at least one of these enterprises, as we shall see, Rikyu was to have an interesting role.

The year 1587 is a memorable one in the history of sukiya architecture. In Kyoto, in that year, Hideyoshi's Juraku-dai was completed, and on September 13, at the age of fifty-one, he moved into it. Just as the construction of his castle in Osaka had marked a turning point for that town and set it on its way to becoming a prosperous city, so the completion of Juraku-dai marked a turning point for Kyoto. Although the name Juraku-dai (Mansion of Assembled Pleasures) suggests that it was only an elaborate residence, it was actually a genuine castle, furnished with a moat, stone walls with apertures for defense by firearms, turrets, a tower or keep, and a two-storied main gate guarded by armed men.

Juraku-dai was surrounded by the luxurious residences of Hideyoshi's retainers. Among them, however, there was one that did not look luxurious at all. Nor did it look commonplace either, since it was a house of extreme refinement and creative distinction. Its owner was Rikyu, arbiter of taste and tea-ceremony teacher to Hideyoshi, and he had built it on land given to him by Hideyoshi within the grounds of Juraku-dai. The house has long since vanished, but an incomplete record of its construction survives, and from this we can get some idea of its appearance.

We know that Rikyu's residence consisted essentially of three rooms, but we do not know clearly the pattern of their arrangement. The first was a room of 18 mats designed for the reception of guests. Adjacent to this was a large room (we do not know its area in mats) featuring a shoin or window alcove with a broad, raised sill designed for use in reading and writing. This feature, it should be noted, gives its name to the style of architecture which employs it as well as to the structure into which it is built, and quite often a room with a shoin is thought of as a study, although it may be used for the entertainment of guests or the performance of the tea ceremony.

Adjoining the two rooms just described was another 18-mat room, and it is this room in which we are most interested, for a modified copy of it exists today, as we shall presently see. Here too there was a shoin window alcove, but the room had other distinguishing features, among them a *jodan* and a *chudan:* raised-floor sections of differing heights for the seating of guests according to social rank. (See floor plan on pages 174–75.) The supporting posts in this room were cut in roughly octagonal shape—that is, first cut square and then irregularly trimmed at the corners: a rustic touch that was taken over from the houses of commoners (minka) and was to become one of Rikyu's trademarks. The woodwork—posts, ceiling, sills, and other elements—was stained with a mixture of *sumi* ink and red oxide of iron, and for this reason the room was known as the Colored Shoin.

In the garden was a teahouse whose floor space was divided into two areas, one of 4.5 mats and the other of 2 mats. A main gate to the compound and two inner gates completed the ensemble of structures. One of these inner gates, standing between the main gate and the house, was a *heiji-mon:* a type of roofless gate with square posts and folding panels which usually served as a symbol of samurai status.

It is clear from the surviving description of Rikyu's house that it was patterned after the samurai residence in *shuden* style. Without complicating matters here by going into too long a digression, we may note that the shuden style represented a transition from the *shinden* style of the nobleman's mansion in the Heian period (ninth through late twelfth century) to the above-noted shoin style, which was perfected around the close of the sixteenth century. Essentially, the shinden mansion consisted of a main building flanked on either side (and somewhat to the front of it) by other buildings, the complex being connected by roofed but otherwise open corridors. A pond at the front was an important part of the setting. The shuden style called for a somewhat more compact arrangement, while the shoin style provided the house with a sizable entryway *(genkan)* and introduced the room with a window alcove along with the tokonoma or decorative alcove in the main room.

When we observe that Rikyu's house on the premises of Juraku-dai was essentially in shuden style, we are taking note in particular of the fact that its Colored Shoin was provided with the raised-floor areas customarily reserved for the seating of feudal lords or other persons of high rank and that its inner gate, the heiji-mon, was a trademark of the samurai residence. Both of these features were symbols of social status in the Momoyama period, but Rikyu, though very rich, was not a samurai. He was a merchant, and the house in which he was born and raised could not have been in samurai style. It must,

Aerial view
of Rinshun-kaku,
Yokohama

三渓園　臨春閣

in fact, have been much like any other prosperous townsman's house in Sakai. Thus we can see that the construction of his house at Juraku-dai was an epoch-making event for Rikyu himself, and we can easily understand why his son Shoan reproduced its Colored Shoin when he established the Senke school of the tea ceremony at the location it still occupies today in Kyoto.

Although Rikyu followed the pattern of the samurai residence in laying out the basic plan for his house, his concepts of design and decoration were completely new and different. The nouveau-riche military leaders of Momoyama and early Edo favored lavish ornamentation, as may be seen in the Ninomaru halls of Nijo Castle in Kyoto and the Audience Hall (transported from Hideyoshi's dismantled Momoyama Castle) at the Nishi Hongan-ji in the same city. Sliding partitions and tokonoma walls were decorated with gorgeous paintings by artists of the Kano school, and ceilings were covered with colorful designs. Intricately carved wooden transoms and highly embellished gables were part of the décor, and gold was used with amazing extravagance, particularly on painted partitions and screens. In the midst of such splendor—and there were undoubtedly many gorgeous halls in the residences of the retainers around Juraku-dai—Rikyu's house must have appeared utterly different, for it rejected all ostentation and gave itself over to the quiet elegance of understatement. Rikyu was not an eccentric, but he was determined to stand firm against the wave of poor taste in design that was now sweeping the country. Briefly, he was resolved to advance his own original and creative ideas of design—ideas based on the aesthetics of the tea ceremony—and his house therefore represented the first expression of the sukiya style.

According to a contemporary record by the writer Yamanoue Soji (his book is called *Yamanoue Sojiki*), Rikyu had adhered faithfully to the old traditions of the tea ceremony until he reached the age of sixty-one, practicing and teaching, for the most part, in the 4.5-mat teahouse built by his master Takeno Jo-o. Then, quite suddenly, he decided to introduce new creative ideas of his own. In 1582, now installed as Hideyoshi's tea-ceremony teacher, he expressed his new ideas in the erection of a 2-mat teahouse for his residence in Yamazaki, on the outskirts of Kyoto. This structure, known as the Tai-an, served as a retreat for Rikyu and apparently was visited by Hideyoshi. Certainly it must also have served as a topic for rather astonished discussion, for we read in Soji's record: "As Rikyu is a master, it is only natural for him to interpret mountains as valleys and east as west. He can ignore the traditions and introduce his own creative ideas, but it would no longer be the tea ceremony if ordinary people imitated him and practiced as he does. Rikyu's tea ceremony is something like a tree in winter. Ordinary people cannot appreciate it, and his style has no meaning except among real masters."

Indeed, Rikyu, after reaching sixty-one, became a creative man. People of his time had a special word for creativeness of the sort that he displayed. They called it *sakui,* or sometimes *sakubun,* and they meant by this both creative ideas and original designing with creative ideas of one's own. Rikyu demonstrated sakui to perfection.

What engendered this creativeness in him was the spirit inherent in the art of the tea ceremony, his aesthetic consciousness, and his opposition to the luxury and flamboyance of the current samurai culture. Because he was a creative man, he enjoyed the freedom of carrying out his own ideas, and for this reason his residence at Juraku-dai did not follow conventional ideas of design. It was not only in the appurtenances of the tea ceremony itself—the chashitsu, the garden, and the utensils—that he was able to express the spirit of this ritual but also in every other element of the residence—the main dwelling, its interior decoration, and the gates. His creativeness, in a word, extended beyond the realm of the tea ceremony to embrace residential architecture as well.

Through this carry-over of tea-ceremony aesthetics into architectural design, Rikyu originated the sukiya style. The succeeding Edo period (1615–1867) was to be marked by an even wider extension of the tea-ceremony influence, which expressed itself not only in architecture but also in garden making, handicrafts, cooking and confectionery, and, by no means less important, manners and general social behavior. In fact, the whole culture of the Edo period was affected by the cult of tea.

To return for a moment to Rikyu's residence at Juraku-dai, it is interesting to note what one of his contemporaries has to say of it. This writer is Sakuma Fukansai (1556–1631), who was exiled to Mount Koya by Hideyoshi's predecessor Oda Nobunaga and who continued to practice the tea ceremony even during the tumultuous period of civil strife that only came to an end when Hideyoshi assumed power. In his *Meigetsushu,* Sakuma says: "It was about the time when Hideyoshi's Juraku-dai was at the height of its splendor. The castle was surrounded by hundreds of houses of feudal lords and retainers, all trying to outdo one another in gorgeousness. Among these mansions there was one that was neither a samurai house nor a house in temple style. Indeed, the house looked somehow historic. The gate had a double roof of tile. The roof of the house was neither too high nor too low, and, unlike the roofs of samurai houses, it had no warp. The pitch was neither too steep nor too gentle. Everything about the house, from gable ends to lattice doors, was different. It is impossible to explain how modest it looked. Truly, it was the house of a well-known tea master. This is the way the house of a commoner should be built."

Sakuma was clearly a keen observer, and his description of Rikyu's house leaves no doubt concerning the creativeness it displayed among the ostentatious but nonetheless conventional samurai residences around Juraku-dai. All the samurai houses, of course, were symbols of social status, and even if there was any room for the expression of individual ideas of design, it was strictly limited by the architectural system employed. In fact, there was practically no room for creativeness at all in such structures. By contrast, Rikyu, except for borrowing the basic plan of the samurai house and allowing himself the foible of one samurai-style gate (undoubtedly because he admired its design), was free of the limitations imposed by status symbols and could thus express his concepts of design without restraint.

Today, in the compound of the Omote Senke school of tea in Kyoto, there is a sukiya-style building which can give us an idea of the architectural taste expressed in Rikyu's house at Juraku-dai. This building, known as the Zangetsu-tei (pages 54–55, 140, 174–75, 182–83), is said to be a copy, although a modified one, of the Colored Shoin in Rikyu's house. We have already noted that Rikyu's son Shoan reproduced this room when he established the Senke school of tea at this location, but the present building is not the original structure of the sixteenth century. It is, instead, a nineteenth-century reproduction, for the Zangetsu-tei was twice destroyed by fire and twice reproduced. Except for a few details, however, the old model has been faithfully copied.

The Zangetsu-tei has a floor space of 12 tatami. (See floor plan and drawing on pages 174–75.) An elevated 2-tatami area (jodan), furnished with a window, occupies one corner. Next to it is a window alcove (shoin) about 6 feet wide. The room is also lighted by other windows on the side opposite the jodan. A square fire pit, covered by a section of tatami when not in use, serves for heating the water for the tea ceremony. Four *fusuma* (sliding partitions) comprise the entrance. The generous window areas give the room an air of brightness, and both the larger space and the abundance of light make the Zangetsu-tei far different in atmosphere from Rikyu's Tai-an teahouse at Yamazaki.

The elevated 2-mat section, the sills of Japanese cedar (cryptomeria) at its two outer edges, and the paulownia-crest pattern of the paper that covers the fusuma and part of the walls are all reminders that the original Colored Shoin at Rikyu's Juraku-dai residence was used for the entertainment of at least one very special guest. And so it was, for Hideyoshi was a visitor there, and the paulownia was his crest.

Although in basic form the Zangetsu-tei is a shoin-style structure, it differs greatly from the shoin-style residences of the samurai. As often seen in teahouse architecture, the jodan sills are of polished cryptomeria in natural shape (stripped of bark but not cut to a geometric pattern), while the supporting posts are of basically square cut with the corners roughly trimmed to produce an octagonal shape. Such posts, approximately 5 inches thick, were never found in the samurai houses of the Momoyama period, for they were considered too slender and unimposing. Usually the thickness of a post in such houses was set at one-tenth of the distance between the center of one post and the next (roughly 8 feet) and was thus about 9.6 inches. Again, in its use of several ceiling styles, the Zangetsu-tei differs widely from the samurai house. In one section, for example, the rafters are exposed to produce a rustic effect, while the ceiling over the jodan is composed of broad natural-grained boards. These features, although regularly used in teahouse architecture, are never seen in the authentic shoin style. Thus the style of the Zangetsu-tei cannot be classified as pure shoin or pure rustic-teahouse style but must be given a designation of its own: the sukiya style.

Strictly speaking, the Colored Shoin of Rikyu's house at Juraku-dai did not represent the sukiya style as we know it today, for its woodwork was painted, while that of the classical sukiya-style building is always left in natural unpainted form. The coloring, as we have observed, was done with a mixture of sumi ink and red oxide of iron, and this method of painting, which allowed a choice of shades through varying the amounts of the ingredients, was commonly practiced in the Edo period, although not in Rikyu's time. Even today, one occasionally finds buildings painted in this way. We may wonder, though, why Rikyu, with his taste for the elegantly plain, painted the woodwork of the Colored Shoin.

One explanation is that he wanted to create a warm and tranquil atmosphere in this room and at the same time to combat the effects of smoke from oil lamps and candles, which in his day were the only sources of illumination. Unpainted woodwork would readily come to look soiled, but if it was first painted red it would eventually take on a rich, dark hazel brown. It seems quite possible that Rikyu foresaw the changes that time would produce in the color and texture of the wood and therefore adopted this coloring technique.

But it is also worth noting that one of the ingredients of the paint, the red oxide of iron, was a rarity in Rikyu's time and was little known among the Japanese. In fact, it was imported from India and was considered to be a precious commodity. Rikyu, being a merchant of Sakai, which was then a flourishing port for overseas trade, naturally knew about this product, and his use of it in painting woodwork was something new and strange. It was, in effect, a demonstration of his sakui, the creative originality for which he was so greatly admired, even though it was not to become a feature of the sukiya style as we know it today.

In the same way the double tiled roof of Rikyu's main gate at the Juraku-dai residence was not typical of the sukiya style as it was to develop in later years. In Rikyu's day the heavy hongawara was the only type of tile used, and we can imagine that his gate looked a good deal more distinguished than those of sukiya-style residences of today, which use a much lighter pantile known as sangawara. The effect of hongawara tiling is grave and imposing, as may be observed in the roofs and gates of Japanese temples, whereas that of sangawara tiling is much simpler and lighter. Rikyu's gate was not as majestic-looking as those of daimyo residences, but it undoubtedly reflected his taste.

Returning now to Shoan's Zangetsu-tei, let us compare it briefly with his father's Colored Shoin at the Juraku-dai residence. To be sure, there are several notable differences. The floor space of the Zangetsu-tei is only 12 mats, while that of the Colored Shoin was 18, and the chudan, the lower of the two raised-floor sections, has been omitted. But the most characteristic features—the sliding-door entrance, the shoin window alcove, and the jodan (the higher raised-floor section)—have been preserved. The basic concept and the essential style are there, and the Zangetsu-tei can serve us as a reliable guide in imagining what the original Colored Shoin was like.

The construction of the residence at Juraku-dai was a memorable event for Rikyu and his family. It came about at a hardly less than glorious time for the man who enjoyed Hideyoshi's favor and had risen to the position of foremost tea master of his day. His house was honored when Hideyoshi came to visit and take his seat on the jodan of the Colored Shoin. But Hideyoshi was a man of unpredictable moods and intentions. Whether Rikyu angered him through behavior that he considered pretentious and arrogant or whether, as another version of the story has it, Hideyoshi was incensed at Rikyu's refusal to surrender his beautiful daughter to him as a concubine, is not clearly known, but the two men became enemies. In 1591, when Rikyu had reached the age of seventy and had lived in his Juraku-dai mansion for only four years, he received an order from Hideyoshi to take his own life. This must have been the reason why Shoan, after his release from the exile to which he was sentenced in the wake of his father's punishment, reproduced the Colored Shoin on a smaller scale, at the same time preserving in his copy the indications that Hideyoshi had once been a guest there.

Today the visitor to the Zangetsu-tei can hardly help being impressed by the refinement of its style. In such features as the cut of the posts, the exposed-rafter ceiling, and above all the simple lines of the room itself, he can observe the fundamental techniques of sukiya construction. If he sits before the jodan, he need no longer view it as a place to seat exalted guests but as a tokonoma: a place for the display of a scroll painting and possibly a flower arrangement or a single art object. He may even take time to wonder what sort of art object would best harmonize with this setting. (The scroll that customarily hangs on the wall behind the jodan today is a portrait of Rikyu himself.) In any event, he can be sure that the Zangetsu-tei, in its nobility of concept and design, is fully qualified to present itself as a pioneer structure in the sukiya style.

2. Cultural Coexistence: The Sukiya Versus the Decorative Style in Momoyama Architecture

Nowadays not only restaurants, inns, various types of public teahouses, and private villas but also ordinary dwellings employ sukiya techniques in their construction. In Kyoto, in particular, we find many traditional-style houses with sukiya features, even though their overall construction is in the minka or commoner's-house style. This might lead to the assumption that a form of sukiya architecture already existed before Rikyu perfected it in the late sixteenth century and that there were many Momoyama buildings similar to the Zangetsu-tei. Such an assumption, however, would be false, and to prove this we have only to recall that Sakuma Fukansai, in his description of Rikyu's house at Juraku-dai, put great stress on its uniqueness. Although many buildings in the following Edo period (1615–1867) showed sukiya influences—among them the Katsura villa (pages 58–59), with its several teahouses, and the Black Shoin of the Nishi Hongan-ji (page 172)—it is important to remember that Rikyu's house was the only building of its time in the sukiya style.

In fact, it was the first sukiya-style building that Rikyu himself designed, even though he had a number of other residences. In the district of Imaichi in Sakai, where he was born and raised, he built a house and a teahouse. He also had a house in the vicinity of Daitoku-ji temple in Kyoto and another on the premises of Osaka Castle, both with teahouses. We know that the teahouses at all of these residences were in traditional tea-hut style—small and unpretentious—and it is safe to say that his dwelling houses were also of conventional form. There is no available record of the house in which he

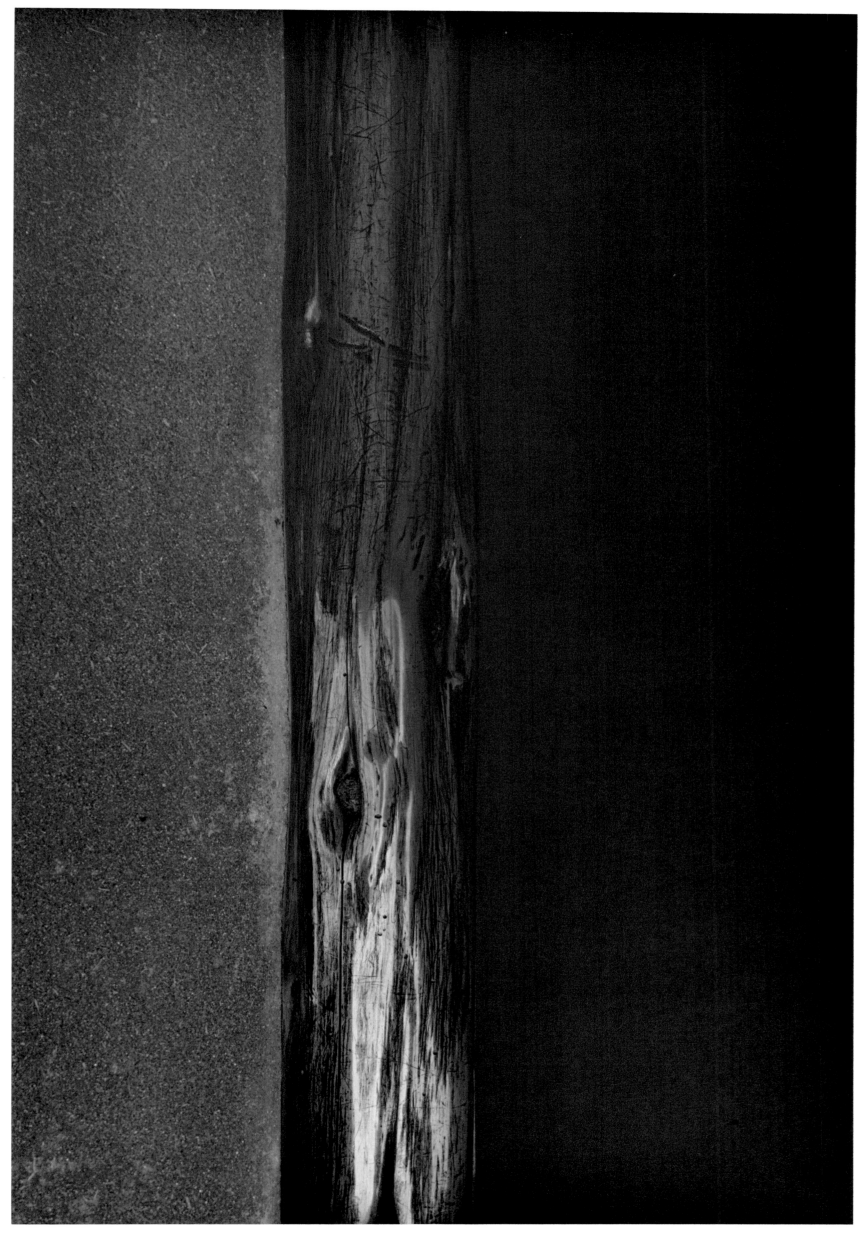

Post and clay wall　皮付きの柱

was born and raised, but it is almost certain that it did not have a room like the Colored Shoin of his Juraku-dai residence. It is natural and therefore reasonably correct to guess that the house was quite similar to other traditional merchants' houses in Sakai.

What were the merchants' houses in Sakai like during the Momoyama and the early Edo periods? Even today there is a saying among the Japanese to the effect that the people of Osaka spend everything they have on food, while the people of Kyoto squander their money on clothes. Until about the middle of the Edo period this adage also included the people of Sakai, who were charged with throwing their money away on their houses. In fact, there was a style of architecture known as the Sakai style, and we can get some idea of its lavishness from the famous novelist Ihara Saikaku (1642–93), who describes it in one of his books. Saikaku notes that careful attention was given to even the smallest details and that much labor (to say nothing of money) was expended on "bamboo verandas, transoms of imported wood, and decorations in gold and silver." "Imported wood," it should be explained, included such luxuries as red sandalwood and ebony, which were brought in from Southeast Asia. Since Sakai was the leading port for trade with foreign countries from the fifteenth through the early seventeenth century, it was quite natural for the wealthy merchants of the town to use imported materials for furnishing and decorating their houses. It would be difficult to find in Saikaku's commentary any indication that the Sakai style exhibited refinements of the type that later marked the sukiya style. On the contrary, Saikaku makes it clear that a taste for gaudiness prevailed among the nouveau-riche merchants of the port town.

Saikaku, of course, was a novelist of the Edo period, and he was writing more than a century after Rikyu was born in Sakai. Consequently, it would be unsafe to assume that the houses of wealthy merchants who were also masters of the tea ceremony were exactly like those that Saikaku describes. Still, when he tells us that the Sakai style represented an "old type of construction, with everything venerable and antique," we may understand that, in Saikaku's time, the houses of the Sakai merchants still preserved some of the flavor of the Momoyama period. It is hardly strange, though, that the houses of townsmen in a flourishing seaport like Sakai should have expressed what Saikaku described as a foreign taste, for the town was flooded with foreign goods.

In their sense of design and decoration the merchants of Sakai, and those of Kyoto and Nara as well, presented an interesting contradiction. We must remember that many of them were masters of the tea ceremony and that they contributed greatly to the development of this ritual, which by their time had acquired a strict code of aesthetics. The simple truth is that they lived in abundantly decorated houses but at the same time created in their chashitsu—their teahouses and tearooms—an atmosphere of elegant simplicity. Thus they followed what might be called a dual concept of design: ornate architecture and decoration for their dwellings and severe restraint for anything that had to do with the tea ceremony. But even if we consider this a contradiction, we must note that it would not have been possible to create chashitsu of beautiful simplicity if they had not been able, on the other hand, to enjoy the cult of gorgeousness. In a word, they had to be men of means to accomplish what they did, and we must not forget that they spent as much money and creative energy on raising the traditional tea hut to the level of art as they spent on luxurious living.

As a matter of fact, it was not only the merchants who displayed this contradiction. Hideyoshi himself was an excellent example of contrasting tastes. At the same time that he was building teahouses in severe traditional style, he also built at least one that is described as having been "made of gold." His castles, mansions, and temples were celebrated for their luxury of design and decoration and, as we have noted before, set the pace for the residences of his retainers. But the love of gorgeous display did not rule out an appreciation of beauty in its more severe forms.

The culture of the Momoyama period was thus marked by the coexistence of two contrasting aesthetic ideals. It is often described as having been gorgeous, brilliant, or baroque, but one may ask whether this covers all of it. Of course it does not, for the castle and the palatial mansion existed along with the unpretentious teahouse, and the teahouse was as much an object of attention and affection as buildings designed to express the power and the glory of their owners. Again, although both the enormous castles and the great mansions of Momoyama were to influence architecture in the succeeding Edo period, the teahouse and the sukiya style that evolved from it were to exert no less influence. In the long run, because it represented the height of excellence in architectural concept and design, it was the sukiya style that prevailed.

It is no exaggeration to say that the creation and development of the sukiya style took place because of the very existence of the Momoyama castle, the lordly samurai residence, and the ornate house of the merchant. Without these, there would have been no contrast, and it would have been difficult to emphasize the cultural importance of the sukiya-style building. In a way the teahouse was a shadow of the luxurious mansion. Without the splendor of the mansion the special subdued beauty of the teahouse and the house in sukiya style would not have been appreciated. Although this might suggest that the disappearance of the brilliant and the splendid in Momoyama architecture would be accompanied by the disappearance of the teahouse also—that the shadow would vanish with the substance—nothing of the sort happened. The two co-existed for a time, but it was the teahouse and the sukiya style that went on to even more significant developments long after the castles and the daimyo and samurai mansions had passed out of fashion and, for the most part, disappeared from the scene.

We may therefore look upon Sen no Rikyu as the first—in fact, the only—person of his time to realize the existence of a gap between the gorgeous residence and the austere-ly simple teahouse and to be aware that both of these architectural styles, as well as the divergent cultural trends that they represented, were in danger of reaching a dead end. Rikyu tried to bridge this gap by giving a special and independent place in the creative arts to the tea ceremony and its architectural setting, both of which might otherwise have vanished with the sunset of Momoyama. Thus he applied his remarkable creative-ness not only to the teahouse but also to the development of a new style of architecture that was in neither the minka, the shoin, nor the shuden tradition—the style, in a word, that is typified in the Zangetsu-tei. As his contemporary Yamanoue Soji observed, the creation of this style was truly a venture in which only a well-known tea master could have engaged. It meant not only a rejection of the highly decorative Sakai style (which itself was to be supplanted by the refined Kyoto style and to disappear a century or so later) but also a firm turning away from the extravagant ornateness of the daimyo and samurai residences.

Rikyu, we should remember, was past sixty when he began to display this new creativeness. He had already reached sixty-six when he epitomized his ideas in the con-struction of his residence at Juraku-dai—the earliest materialization of the sukiya style. Although today we have only the Zangetsu-tei to show us what the Juraku-dai res-idence must have been like, there is no lack of evidence in later architecture to prove the great influence of Rikyu's concepts and innovations. Originating in the teahouse, expanding to include the entire residence, and then going on to find expression in still other structures, the sukiya style itself is a monument to the genius of Sen no Rikyu.

3. Emancipa-tion from the Symbolism of Status

We have seen in the previous chapter how the first residence in sukiya style adopted features of the teahouse some four hundred years ago. We have also noted that, although certain basically shoin-style buildings like those at the Nishi Hongan-ji and the Katsura villa made use of sukiya techniques in the early seventeenth century, the shoin and the sukiya styles are two different things. Again, in an earlier chapter, we have noted that the minka and the sukiya styles are widely different, even though the minka—that is, the houses of farmers and urban commoners—made much use of sukiya techniques as time went on. In the present chapter we shall observe the sukiya style in its role of free-ing architecture from its subservience to the symbols of social status and religious ideology.

It was certainly an epoch-making event for Murata Juko (1423–1502), tea master of Nara and founder of the tea ceremony as we know it today, to introduce the sukiya teahouse as a structure designed for the tea ceremony alone. To be sure, his teahouse had an area of only 4.5 tatami, but it marked the first time that a place had been set aside for this specific purpose. In the latter part of the fifteenth century the shogun Ashikaga Yoshimasa had a 4.5-mat room built into the Togu-do at his Higashiyama villa (famous today as the site of the Silver Pavilion), but this room, called the Dojinsai, was not used exclusively for tea-ceremony purposes. Although it is true that Yoshimasa sometimes used the room for the tea ritual, he also used it as a study, as a place to re-ceive guests, and as a kind of anteroom to the *butsuma,* the adjoining room in which he worshiped before a Buddhist altar. Similarly, before Juko's innovation, there had been the minka-style *chaya,* a structure designed for various types of entertainment, including poetry contests, concerts, and the ritual drinking of tea. But Juko's teahouse asserted its independence of such extra functions and served only the purposes of tea. In doing so, it began the evolution of teahouse design as a form of architecture emancipated from the restrictions of religious and status-symbol architecture.

In the long history of Japanese architectural development from ancient times down to the Momoyama period, there was no age in which the symbols of social status could be separated from the style of construction. The shinden style of the Heian-period nobleman's residence, for example, called for specific types of inner and outer gates, lattice windows, and walls. Regional governors, regardless of how wealthy they might be, were forbidden to incorporate shinden-style elements into their dwellings, no mat-ter how much they might admire shinden lattice windows or how much they might need a wall of the shinden type to harmonize with the design of their gardens or to insure privacy. At one time in the Heian period, under the leadership of the retired emperor Shirakawa (reigned 1072–86), provincial governors in the areas near Kyoto undertook

Jodan (raised-floor section), Zangetsu-tei, Omote Senke school of tea, Kyoto　　　　　　表千家　残月亭の上段の間

a movement to free architecture from some of these restrictions and to obtain for themselves the right to use certain features of the nobleman's house in their own. But their movement failed, and the system of architectural status symbols remained quite rigid, although it is true that the content of the symbolism changed slightly from time to time with the change in building styles.

In Sen no Rikyu's time, social status determined architectural form and style no less than in earlier ages. It was still to do so in the following Edo period. By now the system had become so well organized that it was applied to everything from city planning down to the *kugi-kakushi* (nail covers) used in the decoration of a room. Perhaps the best example of such systematization can be seen in the gate forms specified for the residences of daimyo in the city of Edo (the present Tokyo). It will be both interesting and profitable to stop for a brief look at the regulations concerning gates.

Daimyo who ruled entire provinces were required to construct a *dokuritsu-mon* (literally, "independent gate") with two side entrances in addition to its main one, two guardhouses with gabled roofs, and the lower half of all walls covered with stone. Those of somewhat lower status, who ruled fiefs producing an average of 100,000 *koku* (a koku equaled about five bushels) of rice per year, were assigned the *nagaya-mon* (literally, "long-house gate"), a structure of similar but slightly less imposing style. Daimyo who had been retainers of the house of Tokugawa before 1600, when the first Tokugawa shogun came to power, and whose fiefs produced 50,000 koku of rice, were also assigned the nagaya-mon, but in this case the guardhouse roofs were in different style. Again, daimyo with 50,000-koku fiefs who became retainers of the house of Tokugawa after 1600 (and who had been opponents before) constructed the nagaya-mon, although this variant of the type had only one guardhouse with still a different style of roof. A lattice window was a feature of this form of gate. Lesser lords, depending upon the income of their fiefs and the date when they had sworn allegiance to the Tokugawa shoguns, had appropriately modified styles of the nagaya-mon. Needless to say, for the multiplicity of ranks below these there were yet other forms of gates prescribed according to their social status.

Not only the style of gates but also the style of ceilings within the house, the pattern and color of tatami bindings, and countless other points of design were dictated by the shogunate. No one was allowed to apply in his residence any form of construction design prescribed for those of higher social level than he, or of lower level either. For instance, a Tokugawa retainer who, for reasons of modesty or economy, used a style of gate designated for retainers of lower rank than his own was considered to have disgraced his honor.

Even in the minka, the houses of commoners, a similar system of architecture according to social status prevailed. In Rikyu's time, for example, a style of protruding or extended wall known as the *udatsu* symbolized the houses of leading townsmen who were the owners of estates. Although in later years the udatsu came to serve as protection against fire, in its earlier form it was crowned with a roof of thatch and was thus highly inflammable. But it was a status symbol nonetheless. Similarly, mayors of towns and villages, together with certain other local officials of relative importance, included in their houses the raised-floor areas that we have noted as places for seating guests of superior rank. Since such officials were appointed by the ruling gentry of daimyo and samurai and were required, upon occasion, to receive visits from their overlords, it was necessary for their residences to have proper seating arrangements. But commoners of lower rank than appointed officials were forbidden such features in their houses.

It was the same with almost everything else: the tokonoma and its adjacent closet or shelves, the shoin window alcove, rooms surrounded by verandas, single-panel cedar doors, fusuma with lacquer frames, fusuma with decorations in gold, nail covers, and other features—all were status symbols whose use was strictly controlled. Except in Kyoto, Nara, and Sakai, where pre-Tokugawa traditions somehow prevailed, the rules were rigidly enforced. No farmer, no matter how well-to-do he might be or how much he might have wanted it, was permitted to build a room surrounded by a veranda. Exterior status symbols, such as the ornaments at the ridge of a roof, were strictly regulated as to style and number. Mayors, for example, were allowed more of them than lower-ranking farmers, since the number indicated social rank. The multitude of construction regulations issued by the Tokugawa shogunate is clear evidence of the role that status played in architectural symbolism.

In the stratified society of feudal Japan it was difficult indeed to escape from the rigidity of architectural conventions. Even in the very early period of the great tombs (250–552), however, such conventions existed, for we learn from ancient records that the emperor Yuryaku forbade a provincial governor to use the crossed rafters that we see today on the roofs of Shinto shrines. Such ornaments, said the emperor, could be used only on shrines dedicated to the imperial ancestors. Again, a record informs us that in the fourteenth century, when a new imperial palace was built in Kyoto, the first concern of the designers and the craftsmen was to provide it with the symbols of imperial authority. Although there was more leeway for individuality in the construction of upper-class residences than in that employed for the houses of commoners, the force of tradition was too restrictive to allow more than the smallest expression of creative freedom. Even the military dictators Nobunaga, Hideyoshi, and Tokugawa Ieyasu, who introduced lavishness of color and decoration into their mansions and castles, still followed the basic construction design of the shuden style, which allowed only the very least of real architectural innovation.

What needs to be stressed here is that architectural beauty for its own sake could never be the primary concern of the shoin or the minka style. There is nothing like pure aesthetic consciousness in either of these. So it was also with other traditional styles. To be sure, we cannot deny the existence of beautiful design in Japanese architecture based on social status and religious ideology, but at the same time we must observe that no effort was made, until Rikyu's day, to free this architecture from its limitations and to achieve beauty of design independent of social and religious symbolism. The sukiya style, therefore, was the first to give free rein to creative energy and originality of design.

It was the small and modest teahouse, then, that gave architectural designing its first opportunity to escape from its bondage to religion and a rigid social order. This is an important fact to remember when we consider the characteristics of the sukiya style as they came to be expressed in architecture after Rikyu's time. In the shoin, the teahouses, and the garden of the Katsura villa we can discern not only an intention to pursue true beauty of design but also an expression of the ideals that Rikyu first conceived. The designers of Katsura, Prince Hachijo Toshihito and his son Noritada, although they based their plans on the shoin style, went far beyond the limitations of this style to produce a masterpiece of sukiya architecture. It is interesting, in this respect, to compare the buildings at Katsura with the Ninomaru halls of Nijo Castle, which were constructed about the same time. Although the basic plans of these two complexes of structures are rather similar, the buildings are totally different in appearance. While the Katsura villa displays the beauty of simplicity, the Ninomaru halls are nothing less than baroque in their splendor, and in this contrast we can see two opposite intentions on the part of their respective designers. The Ninomaru halls were designed to impress the citizenry of Kyoto with the power and glory of the Tokugawa shogunate, but Katsura was purely an expression of personal taste: a private villa which had no need to impress anyone except a few select aristocratic visitors, and then only with its owner's discriminating sense of aesthetic values and not with his pomp and circumstance. Modern architecture has nothing to learn from the Ninomaru halls, but it has a great deal to learn from Katsura.

The elegant simplicity of Katsura should not be interpreted as evidence of a passive attitude on the part of its designers. The modesty here is deliberate, but there is nevertheless a full and free expression of the creative spirit—an expression of a kind that had never before been seen in the history of Japanese architecture, not even in the pioneering sukiya structures built by Rikyu. In this sense there is something daring about the style of Katsura, for it opened a world of beauty that no Japanese before its time had ever thought of exploring—no Japanese, that is, except Rikyu himself.

4. Sakui: Creative Originality

In an earlier chapter we noted that Sen no Rikyu was known as a man of sakui—that is, a man of creative originality. It will be worthwhile here to expand a bit on what is meant by sakui, or sakubun, as it is sometimes called. Literally, the word "sakui" means something like "intention" or "conception," but by extension it can be taken to signify originality of creation. Sakubun has the similar meaning of "capability for creation." In Rikyu's time, however, sakui had a more positive meaning than it does today, for true originality of creation was extremely rare in a society which had no record of such startling departures from tradition as Rikyu undertook. In our own time, interestingly enough, sakui has acquired another meaning—although this has occurred through misuse of the word—and we now hear such expressions as "sakui ga medatsu" and "sakui ga katte iru," both of which mean that sakui is too prominent in the design and has produced an effect of artificiality. Nevertheless, in the art of the tea ceremony during the Momoyama period, the creative spirit implied in this word was highly appreciated, and the characterization of Rikyu as a man of sakui was the sincerest form of compliment.

People may tend to think that the sukiya style, once having made use of the virtue of sakui to break down old patterns of architecture, would itself quickly settle into a rigid pattern. It was not until after the middle of the Edo period, however, that the idea of preserving sukiya forms with uncompromising strictness took hold. In the early period of sukiya architecture there were no such formal designations as the Rikyu

桂離宮　書院と池の遠望

style, the Enshu style (named for another tea master), or the Doan style (named for one of Rikyu's sons). Again, even though Rikyu was their teacher, there was great heterogeneity in the teahouse and tearoom styles developed by his pupils—for instance, the tea masters Oda Uraku (brother of the dictator Nobunaga) and Furuta Oribe—for they enjoyed free expression of their individual ideas. This same divergence in sukiya styles can be seen through a comparison between Rikyu's spatial concepts and those of Kobori Enshu (1579–1647), the father of the Enshu style mentioned above. Rikyu favored rather narrow and "closed" tea-ceremony areas, while Enshu was an exponent of the open and the bright. It is important not to misjudge the chashitsu of early sukiya-style architecture by giving too much attention to the conventional chashitsu of the late Edo period. We must remember that during Momoyama times, when Rikyu built his Colored Shoin, tea masters considered it more important to express creative originality —that is, sakui—than merely to let design follow the natural course of things and thereby remain wholly traditional. Because Rikyu and his followers invested the chashitsu with a vital energy—an energy, in fact, that some of their contemporaries found too extreme—this unit of architecture, though small in scale, came to represent a whole philosophy of architectural design and to form the basis for an entirely new style.

The tea masters of Momoyama and early Edo thus looked upon sakui as the *sine qua non* of the tea ceremony and its architectural setting. Here they could be truly creative. The minka and the shoin styles, on the other hand, offered no opportunity for the application of sakui. Even if they had offered such an opportunity, any widespread effort to accomplish creative changes in these styles would have been opposed as a disturbance of the social order and would have been promptly repressed. The sukiya style, however, developing quietly in the shadow of the sanctioned modes of architectural design, served as an outlet for creative energy and originality.

Interest in sakui seems to have existed from the time of Murata Juko, the fifteenth-century tea master whom we have earlier noted as the reputed founder of the tea ceremony in its orthodox form and as the creator of the independent teahouse. We can be certain that this interest continued among the tea masters of Rikyu's earlier days, including his own teacher Takeno Jo-o, even though we have no documentary records to prove it. By contrast, we find an abundance of references to sakui in records dating from the Tensho era (1573–91), when Rikyu had reached old age, to the early Edo period, when Kobori Enshu flourished. The oldest among these records is the previously mentioned *Yamanoue Sojiki*, which appeared in 1589. Its author, Yamanoue Soji, whom we have already met as a commentator on Rikyu and his style, was one of Rikyu's pupils. At the battle of Odawara, in 1590, he had the misfortune to criticize Hideyoshi and to be punished by having his nose and ears cut off. This information is not necessarily irrelevant here, for it offers further proof of the inherent cruelty that led Hideyoshi, the next year, to demand Rikyu's suicide. In any event, it is pertinent to note what Soji has to say about sakui:

"A man who has the ability to discriminate the best and the worst among all sorts of tea-ceremony utensils, who performs the tea ceremony gracefully, and who lives by teaching the tea ceremony is called a tea master. Among men of this type, only those who never use any eye-catching utensils and who are well grounded in the three principles of sakubun, *tegara,* and determined devotion to the art are to be called *wabi-suki* tea masters." Sakubun, as we have noted, is a synonym for sakui. Tegara (literally, "achievement") may be described as "products" of sakui worthy to be treasured by posterity. The idea of wabi-suki (literally, "wabi tea ceremony") is somewhat more difficult to convey, but perhaps the meaning can best be stated as "tea ceremony in subdued or rustic taste." In any case we know that sakui was an essential requirement for the true tea master.

Because there were no textbooks on the tea ceremony in the early days of its history in Japan, men who wished to perfect themselves in the art had to concentrate on whatever records were available. At the same time it was necessary for them to meet with other masters for performance of the ceremony, to learn from them, to study assiduously day and night, and to display sakui in their own conduct of the ritual. Oddly enough, although sakui was a highly prized virtue among the tea masters of Momoyama times, after the middle of the Edo period it was ignored, for by then attention was completely concentrated on preserving the traditional form of the ceremony as it had been handed down from the Momoyama masters.

Sakui permeated every aspect of the tea ceremony, including the dishes to be served as part of the ritual. One record offers this advice: "The menu should be changed at every tea party. The regularly required dishes may be served every time, but unusual dishes should be served every five to ten times. Young tea masters who own traditionally valued utensils may use them over and over, but attention must be given to using utensils that look refined and rustic. Sakui must be displayed not only in the tea-ceremony meal but also in the style of the entertainment, depending upon what time of day the guests are invited to come. Again, it must be displayed in the arrangement of such

◀ Aerial view of shoin buildings, Katsura villa, Kyoto

art objects as hanging scrolls and incense burners. . . . No mere imitation of the sakui of other tea masters is permissible. When distinguished guests are present, a very refined and special sakui must be exhibited." It is clear from this how highly sakui was appreciated, just as it is clear that the copying of other people's sakui was considered reprehensible.

According to the *Kissa Shokuyu Den,* an anonymous book on tea-ceremony traditions published in the seventeenth century, "teahouses and tearooms, which used to have areas of 6, 4.5, or 3.5 tatami, have now been reduced in size to 2.5 or even 1.5 tatami through the influence of somebody's sakui." The unidentified "somebody" here seems to have been Rikyu, and it is clear that Rikyu's pupil Oda Uraku (1547–1621) considered such chashitsu to be the products of sakui. Although Uraku criticized these tiny rooms as being "too small, so that the guests feel shut in," it is certain that they were made small on purpose and not for reasons of economy. In any case we can be sure that they were expressions of sakui.

Uraku's own sakui can be observed in the chashitsu that was formerly part of the Shoden-in, the abbot's quarters at the Kennin-ji in Kyoto, and is now the Jo-an of the Mitsui residence in Oiso, Kanagawa Prefecture. Among the outstanding features of this tearoom are the old calendars used as wallpaper, the triangular floorboard and diagonal wall of the space adjoining the tokonoma, and the lattice window of closely spaced bamboo. Whenever this tearoom is discussed, it is these evidences of Uraku's sakui that claim attention. The lattice window, it is interesting to note, is the ancestor of the type known today as the Uraku window and has long been recognized as a valuable contribution to the art of design.

An amusing story about Rikyu and his wife So-on illustrates still another facet of sakui. Rikyu had acquired the incense burner Chidori (the name means "plover"), which once belonged to the famous fifteenth-century poet Sogi. While he was admiring it, So-on offered the opinion that the legs were too long and that for this reason it looked ugly. Rikyu agreed, for he had been thinking the same thing, and with no hesitation, even though Sogi's incense burner was hardly less than a hallowed treasure, they called in a craftsman to cut the legs about an inch shorter. It is clear from this that one function of sakui was to create beauty where it had not existed before and to do this by means of a delicate but nonetheless strong aesthetic consciousness.

Of no less interest is the fact that sakui was interpreted in terms of "the newer the better." Yamanoue Soji stresses that the accessories of the tea ceremony should be suitable to the times. In this, he may have been repeating what he had learned from Rikyu, but it is certain that sakui was supposed to reflect the fashions of the day and the current circumstances of society. How else could it live up to its own definition as creative originality? The sukiya style, in its early period, demonstrated the dynamic flexibility implied in Soji's emphasis on the new. It was only in Edo times that it became conventional and fixed.

As a corollary to all of the foregoing, we may note that to lack sakui was considered as hardly less than a disgrace in a would-be tea master. The word *fusakui,* used to denote this shortcoming, has the literal meaning of "without sakui." Yamanoue Soji tells us of Tsuji Gensai, ink merchant of Sakai and tea-ceremony pupil of the celebrated teacher Takeno Jo-o, who had mastered every nuance of the ritual but who was a man without sakui and therefore could never be considered a true man of tea. In fact, tea masters like Tsuji Gensai could not really be considered masters at all, and their status was decidedly inferior.

Soji mentions two other tea-ceremony adepts who suffered the same misfortune: Wakasaya no Soka and Fujuan Baisetsu. Soka, like Tsuji Gensai, was a merchant of Sakai, while Baisetsu was a pupil of the tea master Murata Soju. Both of these men, in spite of being extremely proficient in all aspects of the art of the tea ceremony, were criticized for their lack of sakui. The fact that Soji goes out of his way to speak of such cases is in itself proof of the high value put upon sakui.

Up to this point it has been implied that an essential element in sakui is good taste. Paradoxically enough, there is also sakui in poor taste, for it must be remembered that the possession of creative originality does not in itself assure tasteful results. To realize the truth of this, one need only think of a host of modern architectural creations that are certainly original but altogether lacking in taste. In a word, there is always a possibility of creating tasteless buildings in the sukiya style with inexpert sakui. During the early period of sukiya architecture, however, it was more important that sakui be displayed than that it be refined instead of untasteful. Quite naturally, there were failures, but what mattered more than anything else was the expression of a vital creative energy regardlesss of the chances that it might be misapplied.

Originality, then, was of prime importance, and the copying of other people's sakui was always to be condemned. In speaking of such copying, the previously quoted *Kissa Shokuyu Den* has this to say: "Without knowing the fundamental principles, people either imitate or follow with rigid faithfulness the procedures, manners, and variations

Interior of Hasso no Seki, Nanzen-ji, Kyoto

金地院　八窓の席の窓

created by their senior tea masters and take these as the unbreakable governing rules. It is very stupid of them." This, although it applies to the tea ceremony itself, is at the same time a reflection of the philosophy underlying architecture in the sukiya style. Teahouses and other structures of the sukiya type, no matter how beautiful they might be, were not to be copied. The same design was never to be used twice, and repetition was equal to artistic failure.

In brief, the virtue of sakui was highly prized in Momoyama and early Edo times, even though today it is often criticized as leading to artificiality. Indeed, it was sakui that generated the sukiya style. Through its emphasis on individuality it created a new concept of architectural design that was to extend its influence into our own day.

5. Konomi: Design According to Individual Taste

Now that we have defined sakui and stressed its leading role in the tea ceremony as well as in the origin and early development of the sukiya style, it will be worthwhile to look more closely at the forms in which it was expressed, notably in the teahouse, the tea garden, and the appurtenances of the tea ceremony itself. In doing this, it will be convenient to make use of two Japanese terms that are closely related to the idea of sakui. The first of these is *konomi*, which has the literal meaning of "taste" or "preference" but also carries implications, in this case, of original design. The second is *mitate*, which we may define here as "appreciation" but which essentially conveys the idea of discovering new values and functions in old objects and materials and incorporating them into sukiya design. The subject of the present chapter is konomi; that of the following one, mitate.

In the history of Japanese architecture up to the Momoyama period there is no record of any building constructed as an expression of sakui—that is, a building in which the individuality and creativeness of the designer could be readily discerned. Certainly there are famous buildings from earlier times which are closely associated with the names of the people who ordered and supervised their construction—for example, the seventh-century Horyu-ji monastery (Prince Shotoku), the eighth-century pagoda of the Todai-ji (Emperor Shomu), the eleventh-century Phoenix Hall of the Byodo-in (Fujiwara no Yorimichi), and the sixteenth-century *hojo* (abbot's residence) at Daisen-in (Abbot Kogaku)—but in none of these cases was the sponsor the designer. There was no intention to express sakui in these structures, nor would there have been much room to display it even if there had been such an intention, since the architectural forms were dictated by traditional religious and social considerations. Japanese architecture had to wait until the emergence of the Momoyama-period teahouse to find an outlet for individual preferences of design—that is, for the konomi we have defined above.

It is in the sukiya teahouse of Momoyama and early Edo that we first note the association of the designer's name with the style, and here the word "konomi" comes into full play. Among the dozens of examples we may note Rikyu-gonomi (the "k" becomes "g" for purposes of euphony), Oribe-gonomi, and Enshu-gonomi, each of which became a label for the style and preferences of the tea master concerned. It is also interesting to observe that the word had never before been combined with personal names, even though it had been used in other combinations since much earlier times—for example, in *iro-gonomi* (sensuality), the literal meaning of which is "preference for passion." We must remember, however, that the use of such a term as Rikyu-gonomi to describe a certain teahouse does not mean that Rikyu himself built the teahouse. As long as it follows the Rikyu style, it may be called Rikyu-gonomi, for the important thing is the spirit of the design itself. Nor does this mean that an original structure by Rikyu (or any other tea master) was faithfully copied to produce a new Rikyu-gonomi teahouse. In other words it is the essence of a style and its distinguishing features that a label like "Rikyu-gonomi" denotes and not a faultless reproduction of a Rikyu original. The sukiya style, as we already know, did not advance through slavish imitation.

Since a number of the structures illustrated in this book are in the style of famous tea masters and other creative men, it will be pertinent to note them here for the reader's benefit. They are listed with the numbers of the pages on which they (and in some cases their plans) appear. All of them are in Kyoto.

Rikyu-gonomi: Fushin-an (pages 116, 152–53) and Zangetsu-tei (pages 54–55, 140, 174–75, 182–83) of the Omote Senke school of tea; Kan'in no Seki of Juko-in (page 190)
Enshu-gonomi: Hasso no Seki of Konchi-in (pages 62–63, 191, 201); Shokin-tei of Katsura villa (pages 142–43, 162–65, 184–85)
Sowa-gonomi: Teigyoku-ken of Shinju-an (page 173)
Sotan-gonomi: Konnichi-an of the Ura Senke school of tea (pages 70–71)
Nyoshinsai-gonomi: Sa-an of Gyokurin-in (pages 202–3)
Korin-gonomi: Ryokaku-tei of Ninna-ji (pages 85, 132–33, 148, 192–93)

There are, of course, a large number of others, not only at temples and shrines but also in public parks and private residences. Besides these, there are such tearoom forms and styles as the Doan-kakoi and the Sotan-kakoi. Again, as we have noted in the instance of the Uraku window, the names of inventive tea masters have been given to various styles of tokonoma, shelves, and other interior elements; types of tea-garden accessories such as stone water basins, stone lanterns, and gates; and styles of tea-garden design and tea-ceremony utensils. Thus, for example, there are the Rikyu fence, the Oribe tokonoma, and the Enshu lantern. Since Rikyu, Oribe, and Enshu are foremost among those whose names are used to designate such styles, we may take a moment to look at some of the teahouse features that have been distinguished in this way.

In the case of Rikyu we may note the Rikyu-gonomi no seki (tea-ceremony room in Rikyu style), the Rikyu-gaki (a kind of bamboo fence), the Rikyu-doro (a kind of stone lantern), and the Rikyu-kido (a type of bamboo door). Less specifically, we have such designations as Rikyu-meibutsu (tea-ceremony utensils treasured by Rikyu), Rikyu-gata (shapes admired by Rikyu), and Rikyu-gata-monsho (patterns in which Rikyu found beauty). Undoubtedly some of these terms were the inventions of later admirers and had no actual connection with Rikyu himself. Nevertheless, we can see how pervasive his influence was and how far the scope of his inventiveness extended.

Furuta Oribe has given his name to such examples of konomi as the following: Oribe-sanjo-daime (a style of tearoom), Oribe-doko (a style of tokonoma), Oribe-mado (a type of latticed window), and Oribe-doro (a kind of stone lantern). Perhaps better known than these, however, is the pottery called Oribe ware, which he is said to have originated.

The style and konomi of Kobori Enshu are to be seen in the teahouse Hasso no Seki at Konchi-in temple (pages 62–63, 191, 201). The bright and open air created by its numerous windows is an Enshu trademark, and there can be no doubt that he was a man of sakui. He is best remembered for his garden designs, but his name is also memorialized in the Enshu-doro (a type of stone lantern), the Enshu-andon (a cylindrical paper-covered lamp for indoor use), and the ceramic ware called Enshu Shigaraki.

It is surprising to find so many types of teahouses and tea-ceremony adjuncts named for individual masters—to say nothing of shapes and patterns and whole classes of other things that have been given the same honor. Until the Meiji era (1868–1912) this phenomenon in Japanese culture was limited to the art of the tea ceremony and the architecture that it inspired. In an age when architecture adhered more or less strictly to traditional forms, the initiative of the tea masters was something entirely new, and the naming of styles for them was a tribute to their inventiveness and their ability to create refinement in an atmosphere that was stifling with convention and lack of taste.

Although it has already been stated that mere imitation of successful styles and forms was condemned by the advocates of sakui, it must also be explained that copying itself was not generally considered reprehensible in Japanese art and architecture. In fact, it was looked upon as a way of showing respect for the original artist as well as a way of mastering one's own art or craft. Nor were the original artists and craftsmen offended when their works were imitated. The Westerner may wonder why they were so generous with their copyrights, so to speak, and why the imitator was commended rather than denounced. This is not the place for a dissertation on the subject, but we may assume that in the Japanese way of thinking there was nothing of the Western philosophy that art is long and life is short. The wooden sukiya building might serve as a teahouse in the morning and yet go up in smoke in the evening, for fire was an ever present enemy of all Japanese architecture before modern times, just as it is the enemy of traditional-style architecture today. If a building was considered beautiful, it was also considered worth preserving, and quite often in Japanese history preservation meant complete rebuilding according to the original plan. We have already seen how Shoan's Zangetsu-tei was twice burned down and twice reproduced. Admittedly there is something of a paradox here between the opposition of the early sukiya designers to mere copying and the plain fact that copying preserved their style for posterity. But even they, if they were able to say so now, would agree that copying has its virtues too.

6. Mitate: The Discovery of New Values

What is mitate? For the sake of convenience and conciseness it can be defined as "appreciation," but it will be worthwhile here to expand this definition somewhat. Mitate, we may say, is the discovery of new beauty and value in things previously ignored or overlooked and the functional adaptation of such things in new forms or settings. Let us illustrate this with a few examples. When an old stone hand mill, worn out and cast aside in a minka-style house, is used as a steppingstone in a garden, the designer is displaying mitate. When modern sculptors use parts of discarded machinery to create new forms, they are likewise displaying mitate. Needless to say, ingenuity plays an important part in the discovery of such new values and uses.

Shonan-tei teahouse, Saiho-ji, Kyoto　　　　　西芳寺　湘南亭の外観

The tea masters of the Momoyama period were the outstanding exponents of mitate, but even before their time we find examples of the insight they valued so highly. The samurai Furuichi Harima (1459–1508), pupil of the famous tea master Juko, was once attracted by a stone on the roof of a merchant's house in Nara. The stone had probably been placed there along with other stones to hold down the shingles, as is sometimes done on the roofs of traditional Japanese houses. It was not a large stone, but its mountain shape and its coloring—black, with a sprinkling of white at the summit—were particularly pleasing, and Furuichi acquired it from the merchant. This stone, given the name of Zansetsu (Lingering Snow) and used as the central feature of tray landscapes, was to become a famous treasure of the Hongan-ji temple in Kyoto—in fact, one of the most famous stones in Japan. Without Furuichi's discernment, however, it might well have been cast aside when the merchant's house and its shingled roof disappeared. Until Furuichi discovered it, the stone had no tradition and no prestige and, in the eyes of the merchant, no value except the purely functional one of serving as a weight on the roof. Like the Momoyama tea masters, Furuichi was a man of keen insight—that is to say, a man of mitate—and in mitate it is such insight that counts above everything else.

There is a Japanese word, *mitate-e* (mitate pictures or paintings), which is used to describe paintings of historical events done in modern style without reference to the costumes and manners of the period portrayed. (Perhaps *Hamlet* in modern dress may suggest the idea.) In such paintings the incidental historical factors—costumes, manners, setting—are ignored, and the event itself becomes a modern occurrence. Similarly, in mitate there is a sense of trying to discover the "modernness"—or, more specifically, the modern value—in objects which once served different "historical" purposes.

We find still another example of mitate in the stone lantern that almost invariably appears in the teahouse garden. Before the Momoyama period, stone lanterns were found only at Buddhist temples and Shinto shrines, where they served as ceremonial ornaments, or in cemeteries, where they had a memorial purpose. It was the tea masters of the sixteenth century who first brought them into the gardens surrounding their teahouses. Rikyu, we are told, found a special beauty in the lighted lanterns of the cemetery at Toribe and hit upon the idea of placing a lantern of this type in his garden. There is no way of verifying this story, but it offers a good example of mitate nevertheless. In any event, we know that the stone lantern eventually became a necessary fixture of the tea garden.

The tea masters introduced a number of forms of the stone lantern into their gardens. Their greatest inspiration was the Kasuga Shrine at Nara, where even today the lanterns seem almost limitless in number and variety, but other shrines and temples also furnished them with models. Soon there were to be styles of lanterns named for the tea masters themselves, all of them products of the masters' sakui. Among these styles we may note those of Rikyu, Oribe, Uraku, and Enshu, whom we have already met, as well as those of Sowa (feudal lord and tea master, 1584–1656), Choando (tea master and priest of the Kasuga Shrine, 1571–1640), and Ishikawa Jozan (samurai and tea master, 1583–1672).

The mitate spirit was also applied to the selection of tea-ceremony utensils, notably the tea bowls. Particularly favored among tea masters were bowls of Korai and Ido ware, both of which were of Korean origin. Korai bowls were originally made for such household purposes as serving food and washing the brushes used in writing and painting, but the tea masters admired them for their coarse, rustic texture and their honest, unpretentious shapes. Ido ware was of equally plain and humble background, but both Korai and Ido bowls were collected and treasured with a passion that would have astonished their anonymous makers. More interesting still is the high value that the tea masters placed upon features that the potters themselves would have considered flaws: unevenness of texture, cracks in the glaze, odd color effects, and other "accidents" resulting from the firing process. Since such characteristics in the pottery were produced unintentionally and purely by chance, they were esteemed by tea-ceremony devotees. Also, since pottery, like architecture, had tended to emphasize conventional forms—at least until the tea masters began to exert their influence—such recognition of value in the unconventional represented another example of emancipation from the rigidity of social symbolism. Again, if there had been no admiration for conventional forms, it would have been impossible to discover beauty in the unconventional. The contrast here is essentially the same as that between the standard residence of Momoyama times and the teahouse that served as the first inspiration for sukiya-style architecture.

Of the many types of peasant pottery, as we may call it, that emerged in the wake of the tea masters' interest, we may mention such varieties of Korai ware as Azuma, Araki, Iibitsu, and Shioge and such Ido types as Uraku, Kaga, Hosokawa, Rikyu, Roso, Kizaemon, and Sakabe. Some of these, it will be noted, bear the names of tea masters themselves. Almost all of them were made by unknown potters working in the folk tradition.

The most notable product of the mitate spirit was the Momoyama teahouse itself and the sukiya-style architecture that derived from it. As can be readily observed, the sukiya and the minka styles have a number of things in common, and we may say that the sukiya style developed through the application of mitate to the minka style. Nevertheless, it is necessary to note the existence of the minka-style chaya—the structure designed for poetry parties and other forms of entertainment, including the tea ceremony—in the residences of the nobility and townsmen before the sukiya teahouse of the Momoyama period was ever born. Therefore a doubt may arise as to whether the sukiya teahouse of Momoyama inherited the tradition of the chaya rather than that of the minka-style house. We know from an old record that the chaya built at the retreat of the priest Kyokaku in 1469 had shelves of roughly cut wood with the bark left on and that "it looked very rustic." The chaya at the residence of the master Soju, built in 1532, is reported to have had the look of a mountain hut and to have been frequently pointed out as "a subtle place in the town." What was the relationship, then, between the chaya and the sukiya teahouse which Murata Juko introduced in the latter half of the fifteenth century as a structure for the performance of the tea ceremony alone?

Of Juko's teahouse, which we have already taken note of in an earlier chapter, we know that it had an area of 4.5 tatami and that it served solely for the tea ceremony, and we may assume that it differed considerably from the chaya. Of Takeno Jo-o's teahouse, built during the first half of the sixteenth century, we know a bit more. Its basic area was the same as that of Juko's teahouse. It had a thatched roof, a bamboo veranda, and *shoji* (sliding doors covered with translucent paper). We also know that it had a strong resemblance to the shoin style. It was apparently only in Rikyu's time that the teahouse came closer to the minka style. Even though Rikyu's 4.5-tatami teahouse in Sakai made use of certain elements of the shoin style, including a finished ceiling and a tokonoma some two yards wide, it also embodied a number of elements in minka style, such as a *shitaji-mado* (window with bamboo crossbars), an earth-floored entryway, and an ogee-shaped sliding-door entrance called a *kato-guchi*. Of these, the shitaji-mado and the earth-floored entryway are definitely of minka origin.

From all of the foregoing we can conclude that the minka was not the original model of the sukiya teahouse but that first there was created the sukiya displaying influences of the shoin style and that to this, through mitate, were added elements of the minka style. If the construction forms and elements of the minka had been directly copied in the sukiya, there would decidedly have been an atmosphere of *wabi*—that is, rustic taste—but this wabi would have been rather poor-looking and not truly refined. As Takeno Jo-o expressed it, the utensils of the tea ceremony should be like "a fine horse in a stable." In other words, just as the stable should reflect the quality of the horse by being neither too crude nor too elegant, so the sukiya teahouse should reflect the quality of the accessories used in it. The sukiya teahouse, then, was rustic, but it was also refined.

The previously mentioned shitaji-mado will serve as an example of the way in which the sukiya incorporated elements of the minka by adapting them to its own purposes. In constructing the shitaji-mado a part of the minka wall is left unplastered, so that the bamboo understructure of the wall is exposed in the form of a latticed aperture. This type of window had been a feature of Japanese houses since ancient times, but naturally the shitaji-mado of the minka was far more crude than the lattice windows in the houses of noblemen and samurai. According to the *Namboroku,* written by Rikyu's pupil Nambo Sokei and regarded as the bible of the tea ceremony, Rikyu took the idea of the shitaji-mado from the minka for use in his teahouse, but of course it was only the basic idea that he borrowed. It was not his purpose to make a literal copy.

The shitaji-mado of the teahouse (pages 70–71, 152–53) is essentially different from that of the minka. Whereas in the minka a part of the wall is left unplastered to expose the bamboo understructure, in the teahouse the opening is fitted with a loose lattice-work of bamboo different from that used for the wall itself, and the pattern of arrangement is different. The horizontal pieces of the latticework are placed on the inside and the vertical ones on the outside. Sometimes these vertical and horizontal pieces are tied with wisteria vines at the places where they intersect. The window also has a special frame and is fitted on the inside with shoji and on the outside with a bamboo screen or a wooden shutter. Except for the outer bamboo screen, these features are not found in the shitaji-mado of the minka. Thus, although the two types of shitaji-mado are similar in basic style, they are actually quite different in structure. Here we have an excellent example of mitate.

The sukiya teahouse also made use of windows in which a lattice of bamboo was attached outside rather than made an integral part of the wall. This form of window was frequently used in the minka of the Edo period, but it was rarely used in minka before the sixteenth century, and then only as a separate construction of bamboo fitted into the wall and secured with plaster. In the houses of townsmen in the

Shitaji-mado (bamboo-lattice window), Konnichi-an tearoom, Ura Senke school of tea, Kyoto　裏千家　今日庵の下地窓

Momoyama and Edo periods the front latticework was always of wooden bars and had hardly any resemblance at all to the window of latticed bamboo.

We have noted above that one feature of Rikyu's teahouse in Sakai was a kato-guchi or ogee-shaped entrance. Windows of this shape, called *kato-mado,* were also used in teahouses. Since this shape of door or window aperture was originally used in Zen temples and the residences of shoguns, we have here another example of mitate. Naturally, the tea masters played a number of variations on the kato-guchi and the kato-mado through the expression of their creative originality.

We know from the *Yamanoue Sojiki,* the chronicle by tea master Soji which has been cited several times above, that round posts of pine and chestnut, sometimes retaining all of their bark or sometimes part of it, were used in the sukiya teahouse. From the same source we learn that a round, polished piece of cypress was often installed as a *toko-bashira* (tokonoma post). Undoubtedly this style of toko-bashira differed from those used today, and it is certain that no toko-bashira of such style was ever seen in the shoin architecture of the Momoyama period. There were, of course, other types of toko-bashira, including those made of bamboo and those in which the surface was roughly finished by cutting with an adze. Again, such posts were the products of mitate applied to features of the minka, which were adapted and refined to fit the atmosphere of the teahouse. Wooden posts of various designs could be created through the use of the adze—for example, posts showing a wave pattern or those cut to resemble the joints in a section of bamboo. Although the carpenter's plane had come into use in Japan during the latter half of the sixteenth century, the adze was still used for the cutting of posts and beams in sukiya-style architecture. The work was difficult, but only the adze could produce the rustic effects so highly admired by the tea masters.

Naturally there were still other elements of the minka which were incorporated into the sukiya teahouse through the medium of mitate, including, for instance, styles of walls and ceilings, but it must not be thought that everything in the minka style commanded the tea masters' admiration. They selected only those elements which they considered to be examples of basically good design and in which their keen discernment found aesthetic value. That is, they borrowed from the minka only those aspects which could be improved and refined through their sakui—their own creative originality.

7. The Sukiya Style Versus Status-Symbol Architecture

We have already observed how the sukiya style developed out of a desire to escape from the limitations imposed upon architecture by religious ideology and concepts of social rank. In essence, the style represented a turning away from status-symbol architecture and the attainment of new creative freedom, but this is not to say that sukiya techniques, for all their individuality and variety, could be incorporated into buildings whose form was dictated by social traditions. Shrines, temples, and the residences of daimyo and samurai, for example, were required to follow prescribed patterns and could admit no deviations of the sort that the sukiya style delighted in. And since these formal structures were located on the main streets during the feudal period, the sukiya style was limited to back streets and more out-of-the-way places. Sometimes purely charming, sometimes dignified and noble, and sometimes quite modest, this style rejected traditional formality and the rigid restrictions of conventional architecture.

To understand how conventional architecture must necessarily refuse admittance to sukiya techniques, we may look for a moment at the typical samurai or daimyo residence. The front and central parts of the structure served for such purposes as the reception of official guests (in some cases even the shogun), the holding of meetings and conferences, and the performance of other official duties. There was no room here for the introduction of new techniques, since everything was subject to strict architectural conventions. The size of the posts and the style of the ceilings, for instance, were determined by these conventions and could not be changed, for they, like all other aspects of the building, symbolized the status of the owner. For this reason the only buildings in which sukiya techniques could be employed were those in which no status symbols were required—buildings, that is, like private villas and retreats.

Among surviving residences of this type is the elegant shingle-roofed villa built during the Empo era (1673–80) by Matsudaira Yorishige, lord of Sanuki Province (the modern Kagawa Prefecture) in Shikoku. Today it stands in Ritsurin Park in the city of Takamatsu (pages 144–47). One of its most notable sukiya features is the diagonal arrangement of its floor plan (pages 88–89), which permits a view from all sides of the component structures and assures a maximum of ventilation in the oppressive heat of the Japanese summer. The villa actually consists of two main parts, the Shoen-kan and the Kikugetsu-tei, but these are joined only at one corner instead of being integrated under a single roof. The broad verandas on all sides, the rather weightless look of the shingled roofs (as contrasted with the heavy look of tile roofs), and the general openness of the construction give this sukiya-style villa an air of lightness and grace that no samurai's official residence ever displayed.

We may note several other examples of sukiya-style buildings of the villa or retreat type that survive from earlier times. The Rinshun-kaku (pages 46–47), originally built as a villa for the lord of Kishu Province (the present Wakayama Prefecture), now stands in the Sankei-en garden in Yokohama. On the premises of the Enuma Shrine in Daishoji, Ishikawa Prefecture, is a small sukiya-style house that was built in 1709 for the lord of Daishoji and once stood in his castle compound. It comprises one 6-tatami room surrounded by a veranda about 2 yards wide, an entranceway, and an earth-floored area. The Kobun-tei of the Kairaku-en garden in Mito (Ibaraki Prefecture), built by Tokugawa Nariaki in 1842 as a place for public recreation, is another sukiya-style structure that has been preserved to the present day.

Regrettably, the Yoko-kan of the Matsudaira residence in Fukui City was destroyed during the Pacific War, but it is worth noting here as a typical example of the sukiya-style retreat of the early Edo period. It was a fairly spacious structure built beside a pond. (See floor plan and elevation on pages 150–51.) Its seven rooms included a *gyoza-no-ma* (literally, "seat-of-honor room") for the reception of particularly distinguished guests and a *tsukimi-no-ma* (moon-viewing room). Outside the moon-viewing room was a dry-landscape garden, and across the pond stood a teahouse named Usu no Chaya (Teahouse of the Hand Mill). Since the designer of the Yoko-kan and its garden was the tea master Yamada Sohen (1627–1708), it was quite natural that the ensemble should display a variety of sukiya techniques, even though the main Matsudaira residence adhered to the canons of status-symbol architecture.

The same tendency to employ the sukiya style in nonofficial architecture (as we may label it) could be seen in the nonpublic parts of temples and the strictly private establishments of the court and the nobility. At the Nishi Hongan-ji in Kyoto, for example, the Shiro Shoin (White Shoin), originally built as an audience hall for the shogun Tokugawa Iemitsu, is not only in typical shoin style but is also lavishly decorated with carved woodwork and gorgeously painted walls, sliding partitions, and ceilings. On the other hand, the Kuro Shoin (Black Shoin) of the same temple served a purely private residential purpose and could thus incorporate an abundance of sukiya techniques. The reason why the Katsura villa could make extensive use of the sukiya style is that Prince Hachijo erected it as a private and nonofficial residence. No matter how critical he might be of the contemporary feudal culture or how enthusiastically he might be devoted to the art of the tea ceremony, his official Kyoto residence at Imadegawa could not have been built in the sukiya style. In a word, his prestige as an imperial prince forbade any such departure from conventions.

For the same reason the buildings of the Shugaku-in imperial villa (pages 134–35, 180–81) employed the sukiya style. Shugaku-in was built as a retreat for Emperor Gomizuno-o (1596–1680), who, even after his forced abdication in 1629, was still required to maintain an official palace in standard court style. His admiration for the sukiya style could be expressed only in building a purely private retreat, and Shugaku-in survives today as a monument to his discriminating taste and excellent sense of design. Similarly, the samurai Ishikawa Jozan (1583–1672), after being forced into retirement, built himself a retreat in the hills behind Kyoto: the hermitage named Shisen-do, which remains today as a landmark of early sukiya-style architecture.

For men of high position, the less their official residences were permitted to differ from those of their peers, the more they desired to express their individuality in villas and retreats in the sukiya style. Undoubtedly this was one way of escaping from the psychological pressures of a rigidly ordered society. It is extremely interesting to note, apropos of individuality, that among these early sukiya-style buildings there is none that closely resembles another in its floor plan. The rooms were arranged quite freely according to the taste of the clients, and there is nothing like a standard or basic form of layout. The official residence of the nobleman and the warrior, as we have seen, was laid out in accordance with his status. The abbot's chamber in a Zen temple always consisted of six rooms arranged in a prescribed pattern. The main hall of an emperor's palace strictly followed a traditional plan. But construction in the sukiya style followed no fixed plan at all. The only guide was individual taste.

It did not take long for the sukiya style to expand widely in plebeian architecture. Such a development was quite natural, for the tea ceremony had achieved great popularity by the late sixteenth century, and it was the tea ceremony, of course, that fathered the sukiya style. Although it was not for this reason alone that sukiya techniques infiltrated the architecture of the common people, the influence of the tea ceremony on the general culture must not be underestimated. To learn this ritual was not only to learn how to drink tea in an aesthetic atmosphere; it was also to learn manners and to achieve

Section of facade, Ichiriki-tei, Kyoto　　一力亭の格子と犬矢来

social grace. Parents expected their daughters to master a whole code of etiquette through their tea-ceremony lessons. Artists and writers, prosperous merchants, and even warriors adopted the cult of tea both for its own aesthetic virtues and for its cachet of social correctness. Artisans—for example, potters, bamboo craftsmen, and woodworkers—reflected the preferences of the tea masters in their products. Even confectioners felt the tea-ceremony influence, for they began to copy the cakes created by the masters to serve as tea-ceremony refreshments. In flower arrangement, rigid traditional styles gave way to the much less formal and much more simple styles used in the tearoom. It was the same in garden design, for now it was the tea garden that people began to copy rather than the dry-landscape garden of the Zen temple, which had served as a model before.

Again, it was the same in architecture. The front and formal parts of commoners' houses—for example, the houses of town and village mayors, landowners, and shopkeepers (in which shop and living quarters were combined)—were no less subject to the status-symbol concept than were the residences of the upper classes, but the rear and purely private sections offered wide possibilities for the employment of sukiya techniques. In fact, it was here that many elements of the minka were improved upon and refined through mitate, the "discovery of new values" that we have earlier noted as an essential factor in the creation of the sukiya style. Thus the sukiya influence produced an improvement in minka design. One example of such improvement is the shitaji-mado, the latticed window described in the previous chapter. Another is the so-called Juraku wall, which was a common feature of houses in Kyoto.

Clay from Juraku, the Kyoto area where Hideyoshi built his castle Juraku-dai, was much favored for the construction of walls in commoners' houses. It was the creators of the sukiya style, however, who found exactly the right combination of Juraku clay, sand, and other ingredients to produce a charming texture. When they wanted a darker shade, they added clay from the Jujo district of Kyoto. By thus refining the commonplace Juraku wall and employing it as an element in sukiya architecture, the designers not only showed a keen eye for values but also elevated a feature of the minka to distinction.

It was the more public buildings, however, that gave the fullest expression to the sukiya style in the architecture of the commoners. Generally these were places of entertainment, and they included teashops, restaurants, inns, *machiai* (geisha assignation houses), and *ageya* (places where geisha entertained their customers in private). Through their interpretation of sukiya concepts and techniques, these buildings achieved a characteristic beauty of their own. For the sake of convenience we may group them all under the heading of chaya, which, although it literally means "teahouse" and has been identified in an earlier chapter as a structure for entertainment in private residences, embraces a considerable variety of public and semipublic establishments. Among these we may note, in addition to those listed above, the *ryotei* or *ryori-jaya* (elegant restaurants at which geisha furnished the entertainment), *sumo-jaya* (restaurants with sumo wrestlers as entertainers), and the *shibai-jaya* (theater restaurants or restaurants with actors as entertainers).

Until the sukiya influence began to assert itself, all chaya were in the minka style. In the feudal period, however, the public chaya were strictly confined to designated localities, since the enterprises carried on in them were generally considered vulgar. In Edo, in particular, the gay quarters and the theatrical district were separated from the rest of the city by walls and moats. Sometimes these chaya districts grew up around shrines and temples, where the magistrates were less strict than those in other parts of the cities. We can find examples of this in such celebrated Kyoto districts as Shimabara, Gion, and Ponto-cho and in the notorious Yoshiwara of Edo. Nevertheless, these areas were considered separate entities.

The patrons of the chaya, however, were by no means the commoners alone, for samurai and other men of high social rank, even though the strict ethical code of their class forbade such mingling with the masses, were frequent customers of these establishments. Usually they went in disguise, or at least under assumed names, and thus there developed a kind of democracy of the entertainment districts in which samurai and other persons of standing, merchants, artists, actors, and the ordinary citizenry met on equal terms. Here men of wealth and social status could escape from the pressure of the code that dictated almost every aspect of their daily lives. Here they could also escape from the formality of the residences in which they were compelled to live, and we may be sure that the owners of the chaya took full advantage of this by constructing their buildings in an appealing style—in a word, by making them as attractive as possible to their wealthy patrons. This style, of course, was the sukiya style, which had already established itself in the villas and retreats of feudal aristocrats and had thus demonstrated the great charm that it held for them. It is hardly surprising that the chaya, in turn, became models for the houses of ordinary townsmen and thus motivated an even wider adoption of the sukiya style.

During the eighteenth century, chaya and large inns became the scene of tea-ceremony performances and flower-arrangement exhibitions. An old record describing
a flower-arrangement exhibition held in 1762 at the Ogiya, a chaya in the Asakusa
district of Edo, informs us that the guests enjoyed the show, "sitting on red carpets,
drinking sakè, and eating fine food." But it was not only to look at flowers and practice the tea ceremony that people went to the chaya. They were also attracted by its architecture and eventually began to copy it. They had heard, of course, that there
were superb shoin rooms in the mansions of the aristocracy, but these they were
never permitted to see, and the shoin style could thus have no influence upon them
whatever. Regardless of how wealthy a commoner might be, he could not enter the
residence of a samurai or a daimyo, but even people of limited means could visit
a chaya and appreciate its architectural charms. Better still, they could enjoy its atmosphere of refined and elegant beauty, and this beauty, we hardly need add, was quite
superior to that of the interiors which social custom forbade them to see. It was the
aesthetic inspiration of the chaya that brought the sukiya style to popularity and
made it symbolic of the architecture of the common people. Again, the inaugura-
tion of the sukiya style was the only development in feudal-period architecture that
transcended the limitations of the class system. The samurai and the daimyo, in
building their villas and retreats in the sukiya style, found a way of escape from the
inhumane restrictions of the shogunate, while the townsmen and other commoners,
adopting the same style, found an outlet for their creative aspirations and an escape
from their own sense of oppression.

8. Characteristic Sukiya Techniques and Materials

In developing the sukiya teahouse and other types of buildings derived from it, the tea
masters applied the principle of sakui in a great number of ways and thereby produced a considerable number of variations. Regardless of variations, however, there
were certain common elements of structure and design, for the concept of sakui was
always controlled by the equally important concepts of *wabi* and *sabi*. These terms,
though difficult to define in any precise way, may be taken to mean something like
"rustic simplicity" and "flavor of age" (or perhaps "patina of age"). In a word,
creative originality was to be expressed within the limits of the rustically simple and
the attractively antique. To put this more concretely, the teahouse, no matter how
much it made use of originality and no matter how new its materials might actually be,
must appear no more brash and new than the paraphernalia of the tea ceremony itself.
Just as it was better that the teakettle be a bit rusty, so it was better that the teahouse have a certain look of age, even though its materials themselves might not
be old. Again, although originality was prized, it was a most selective originality.
In our previous glance at the tea masters' adaptations from the minka, we observed
that not all the elements of the minka inspired them with admiration and that they
chose only those which fitted their concepts of design. The sukiya teahouse thus represented a transfer and enhancement of values found in already existing architecture,
but it did not represent a repudiation of all previous structural techniques and materials. In the present chapter we shall see how the sukiya style molded these techniques
and materials to its own purposes.

Essentially, a sukiya-style building is a construction of straight lines, and in this
respect it does not differ from other traditional Japanese styles, although, of course,
curving roofs often cover straight-line buildings, as in temples and shrines. Both
the floor plan and the elevations of a sukiya-style structure display the beauty of
straight-line composition. It should be noted that load-bearing walls have no place
in traditional Japanese architecture as they do in the stone or brick architecture of the
West, the chief reasons for this being the prevalence of earthquakes in Japan and
the preference of the Japanese for opening up the sides of their houses to let
nature come in, so to speak, and to permit free circulation of air during the hot and
humid summers. Briefly, the post-and-beam system is the essence of traditional Japanese architecture, and wood is the principal material.

It is only natural, then, that traditional architecture in Japan should have emphasized
the characteristics of wood: its tenacious strength and at the same time its softness,
its versatility, its textures, and its natural colors (since it was practically never painted,
either in exteriors or in interiors). The well-developed tenon-and-mortise system of
Japanese architecture, with all its variations, could not have evolved in construction
based on such materials as brick and stone, for there would have been no need of it,
and thereby an important element of architectural beauty would have been lost.
Nor would Japanese construction have been able to display the lightness and grace
that characterized so much of it, particularly after the introduction of the sukiya style.
To repeat, wood in straight-line construction forms the basis of sukiya architecture.

This is not to say, however, that the curve has no place in the sukiya style. We have

Reed-and-bamboo ceiling　葭簀張りの天井

already noted the ogee-shaped window and door, and we may also note the perfectly circular window (pages 186–87) as well as the arched doorway (page 191) and window (page 37). The tokonoma post and the transom may also display curves. All these, however, must be considered accents to the basic straight-line composition.

To achieve harmony in this straight-line composition, the sukiya designers of Momoyama and early Edo used the tatami as a basis for determining measurements and proportions—first for the floor area and then for all other elements of the building. Although the size of the tatami varied from region to region and from period to period, it was the *kyo-ma-datami* or Kyoto-style tatami that became the standard for sukiya construction. The area of the Kyoto tatami, approximately 6.26 by 3.13 feet, was considered as a grid of 36 units, each measuring about 1.04 by .52 feet, and all measurements were decided in terms of these units. Thus the size of the shelves, for example, would represent a certain number of the 36 units of the tatami. In a word, the tatami and its 36-unit grid became the module for all elements of the structure and for all spatial arrangements.

We learn from old records that Rikyu did his planning in terms of rectangles derived from the tatami grid. We are also told, although there is no evidence to prove it, that the modular system based on the tatami was invented by Noami (1397–1471), the connoisseur of art objects who served the Ashikaga shoguns Yoshinori and Yoshimasa and wrote a celebrated book about the treasures in their collections. Even if it is true, however, that Noami introduced the system, it is also true that the size of the tatami in his day varied from room to room, and it was not until the Momoyama period, when the size become more or less standardized, that the system achieved genuine functional importance.

The use of straight-line composition in buildings of the sukiya style does not mean that the arrangement of the rooms follows a square or a rectangular plan like that, for example, of the traditional Western box-shaped house. Nor does it mean that the elements of these rooms are all quite regularly placed—like the windows, let us say, of the usual office building. In fact, it is the diagonal line that rules in sukiya planning, not only in the arrangement of the rooms and their elements but also in the approach to the building itself.

Two excellent examples of this diagonal-line arrangement of component structures can be seen in the plan of the Kikugetsu-tei and Shoen-kan in Takamatsu (pages 88–89) and the aerial view of the Rinshun-kaku in Yokohama (pages 46–47). The diagonal-line approach is perhaps best illustrated at the Katsura villa (pages 58–59, 112–15), where it is employed in several different ways.

The advantage of such diagonal-line arrangements are numerous. In the case of the diagonal approach, for example, one is not presented with a head-on view of the house but perhaps only a glimpse of it through trees and shrubbery and thus may enjoy the changing views as he moves from the gate to the main entrance. The element of curiosity is also involved, since the house does not fully reveal itself until one arrives immediately in front of it. The principle of the diagonal line may also be used in the corridors which connect buildings arranged in typical sukiya-style sequence, and the psychological effect is much the same: changing views and pleasurable anticipation.

The diagonal-line arrangement of component structures—that is, rooms which are actually separate entities but are linked together only at one corner—offers the major advantages of views from all sides and maximum ventilation in summer. At the same time it allows for more light from outdoors. Its psychological and aesthetic advantages are obvious, and we need only look at the illustrations in this book to see what they are. Among the sukiya-style designers we have already met, it was Kobori Enshu who particularly delighted in the freedom and openness of such construction.

Interestingly enough (and as we might have suspected), the diagonal-line arrangement—or irregular arrangement, as we may call it—originated in the tea ceremony itself. Since any square or rectangular marshaling of the tea-ceremony utensils was considered both unoriginal and unaesthetic, the tea masters arranged them in a basically triangular formation. Similarly, an irregular placement of the teahouse windows was favored (pages 62–63, 152–53, 202–3).

In all of this—the arrangement of tea-ceremony utensils, the placement of windows, the diagonal-line approach from gate to main entrance, the staggered sequence of buildings—we can observe the love of asymmetry that again and again finds expression in Japanese design. The strictly symmetrical has no surprises, admirable though some of its expressions may be. This is not to say that the Japanese ruled out all considerations of symmetry, for most certainly they did not, as a great deal of Japanese design makes clear. It is to say, however, that an appreciation of asymmetry enabled them to create designs capable of arousing curiosity and pleasure, both in their art and in their architecture—and most notably in the development of the sukiya style.

For its basic material, as we have observed, the sukiya style uses unpainted wood. Unlike the minka style, which may use such pigments as yellow ocher, red oxide of iron, and sumi ink to color its woodwork, the sukiya prefers to emphasize the characteristic beauty of the material itself. Nevertheless, wood is not used in purely natural form—that is, just as it is cut from the original logs. First there must be a strict inspection for quality and grain, and this is followed by laborious polishing to bring out the latent beauty of the material. Needless to say, the wood must be selected with a good deal of discernment if it is to produce a distinguished effect in the construction. Ordinary unpainted posts, for instance, can be found anywhere in Japanese architecture, but the sukiya designer cannot be satisfied with such prosaic materials. If he wants fine-quality cryptomeria, it must come from such places as Kitayama in Kyoto or the Yoshino region in Nara Prefecture, for just any cryptomeria wood will not do. The same is true of all other types of wood used in sukiya-style construction: quality comes first.

The finishing process must serve the purpose of revealing rather than covering up the natural virtues of the wood. The aim is not a faultlessly smooth surface like that of a hardwood ballroom floor or a gleaming mahogany desk, but the process is time-consuming nonetheless. Two examples will demonstrate this more concretely.

The polished logs used for tokonoma posts, beams, and rafters are often of Kitayama or Yoshino cryptomeria. After the rough outer bark has been peeled off, they are polished with white sand or with another variety of fine sand wrapped in leaves of hemp palm. A second polishing is done with rough straw rope. To the eyes of the amateur the logs may look as if they had merely been peeled, since the polishing has not obliterated their original shape, but of course much labor has gone into the process.

Bamboo, which is also used for posts as well as for ceilings, requires no less painstaking treatment. It cannot be simply cut and brought into the construction as it is. To begin with, it must be cut at the proper time in order to avoid infestation by insects. Next, it must be steamed to eliminate the oil, given several preliminary polishings, and allowed to age until its color changes from green to light yellow. Only then can the final polishing and installation take place.

The tea master Yamanoue Soji, who has been cited as an authority several times before in this book, was quite right in observing that the sukiya style, although it treasured the color and texture of raw materials, never actually used raw materials in the true sense of the word. In fact, the natural and rustic look of these materials is achieved only at the cost of a great deal of labor and money. If we were not particular, if we objected to spending and money, and if we therefore brought in a piece of Japanese red pine straight from the mountains as a tokonoma post, the room in which we used it would look nothing but cheap and untasteful.

9. The Refinement of Detail

While it is true that the sukiya style adopted the details of the teahouse with great enthusiasm—posts, ceilings, walls, windows, shoji, fusuma—it is no less true that it subjected these details to much refinement. It is also true that it turned away from the basic tradition of the teahouse. For example, it retained the shoji but at the same time it threw its rooms open to the outdoors instead of striving for the closed atmosphere that Rikyu and other earlier tea masters preferred. To be sure, it may be said that the sukiya style, in thus rejecting closed areas, rejected a feature that expressed the very essence of the classical tea ceremony. Similarly, it may be said that if the traditional teahouse was characterized by a certain quality of mystery—a kind of abstruseness, perhaps—the sukiya style was by contrast bright and refreshing. Again, if the elements of the teahouse represented a refinement of elements from the minka, then we can say that those of the restaurant, the assignation house, and the private villa constituted yet another refinement, with the teahouse standing midway between.

We have already noted the great care with which posts and beams are selected and finished for use in the sukiya-style building. In the minka such elements tended to be large and roughly finished, but there, of course, their tough vitality was appropriate to the sturdy structure. In the teahouse these members were smaller but hardly less rustic. In the sukiya-style building they took on a new lightness and grace and an air of greater sophistication.

Ceiling styles were developed in great variety, and several styles might be employed in a single room, as we have seen in the example of the Zangetsu-tei. Wood was only one of the materials, for paper, straw mats, reed, and bamboo were also used. Board ceilings of numerous types appeared, including those in which the rafters were exposed to create a more interesting effect. Beams and rafters might be of bamboo in sections of varying diameter or of cryptomeria, pine, or cherry, sometimes in natural form and sometimes cut in different geometrical shapes.

The clay wall of the minka, a survival from the clay houses in which the common people lived in early times, was taken over by the sukiya style and refined into an important structural element. It is interesting to observe, in this connection, that clay was never used as a building material by the nobility in earlier days but that, after the advent of the sukiya style, it appeared in the houses of noblemen as well as those of commoners. In addition to the Juraku wall described earlier in this book, there was the wall made of Juraku clay and red oxide of iron, a combination that produced the warm tone of red seen today in the walls of such Kyoto landmarks as the Ichiriki-tei restaurant and the Ijaku-tei of the Nishi Hongan-ji.

Paintings on walls and fusuma, which are often seen in shoin-style buildings, had no place in the sukiya-style building. In the first place, such adornments were considered unsuitable to the aesthetic atmosphere of the tea ceremony and, by extension, to the sukiya style. In the second place, it was practically impossible to paint on the type of clay wall favored for the teahouse. This fact, however, was irrelevant, since it was the clay itself—its color and its texture—in which the sukiya designers were interested and not its appropriateness for mural decoration. In some instances, when the clay was particularly fragile and subject to damage—specifically, the lower section of the walls—it was covered with paper to a height of several feet. Various kinds of strong handmade paper were used. In some instances, as in the Konnichi-an of the Ura Senke school of tea, pages from old records or calendars were used to create a special effect and a pleasant contrast between the white of the paper and the color of the clay (pages 70–71). In other cases, wallpaper of special patterns was used to cover whole areas of clay—for example, the paulownia-crest paper which we have noted in the Zangetsu-tei.

Shoji—the sliding panels of wood and translucent paper that serve more or less as exterior walls in traditional Japanese houses—were not an invention of the sukiya style, for they had already existed in residences and teahouses since earlier times. The sukiya designers, however, took every advantage of their possibilities and used them with considerable versatility. One example will be enough to demonstrate the importance of the shoji to the sukiya style.

In the minka it was customary to provide one section of the shoji with a small sliding panel of its own to allow the family cat to go in and out. This *neko-ma-shoji* (shoji with an opening for the cat), as it was called, developed into the *yukimi shoji* (snow-viewing shoji), a type of shoji with glass panels at the bottom and vertically sliding sections which could be raised to give a view of the outside without opening the shoji themselves (pages 34–35). This arrangement, of course, is designed for wintertime use, so that the outdoor scenery can be enjoyed in comfort, but a good deal more than just this physical factor is involved. It may be interesting to look for a moment at the aesthetic principles that have a part in this.

The Japanese do not think of the shoji door (or window) as a divider between interior and exterior, even though it does serve this purpose. They see the shoji, rather, as a means of uniting indoors and outdoors. In the case of the yukimi shoji, when the glass panels are covered, nothing can be seen but the shadows of trees and shrubbery or perhaps the patterns created by reflections of sunlight on the garden pond. Nevertheless, the outdoor scenery can be imagined, since it is symbolized by the shadows and reflections. It may even be idealized through such imagining. In any event, the sensation is an aesthetically pleasurable one. Similarly, if the sliding sections are lifted to give a view of the outside, one sees only a portion of the garden and none of the sky, and thus there is an illusion of a greater area than that which actually appears. Now, if the weather is no longer cold, and the shoji themselves can be pushed open or removed (as in the heat of summer), the room will be filled with sunlight and fresh air, the whole garden will be in view, and indoors and outdoors will be integrated. In summer, blinds of split bamboo may be hung in the openings to subdue the light (pages 42–43), and the garden may be sprinkled to create an illusion of coolness. The versatile yukimi shoji thus perform an important function in creating the atmosphere of the room.

Like the shoji, the sliding partitions called fusuma were not an invention of the sukiya style but were adapted by the sukiya designers to their own purposes. In the shoin style, as we have noted, the fusuma were often ornamented with paintings, but in the sukiya style they were kept quite plain or at most decorated with unobtrusive patterns, as they still are today. It was not their function to call attention to themselves through their gorgeousness. Their colors were almost always white or such quiet tints as light green, pale lavender, light blue, or reddish brown. In contrast with the brilliantly painted fusuma of the shoin style, those of the sukiya style had a distinctly modern look.

In their adaptation of the tokonoma, as in their other borrowings from earlier architectural styles, the tea masters created a number of variations. The shoin-style tokonoma, being no less subject to the canons of status-symbol architecture than any other feature of the shoin-style building, could only follow a prescribed pattern, and any alteration of its form would have been considered a violation of propriety. In the sukiya style, however, since such restrictions did not apply, the tokonoma could display great freedom of design. The only requirement was that it must still perform, or at least suggest, the role it played in earlier architectural styles: that of serving for the seating of the main guest, whose position was, in the beginning, in the tokonoma itself and, in later times, in front of the tokonoma post. Through the liberation of the tokonoma from the strait-jacket restrictions of the shoin style, not only guests in private residences but also patrons of restaurants and inns could have the pleasure of discovering new and interesting versions of an old established form. And the sukiya designers, needless to say, had the even greater pleasure of indulging their creative originality.

The tokonoma post, as an element of prime importance, followed the changing style of the tokonoma itself. In shape, it might be square or round or beveled at the corners. It might be a straight-cut section of wood or a tree trunk in natural form, stripped of bark and polished. Favorite types of wood for the tokonoma post included Japanese cypress, pine, maple, red sandalwood, ebony, Indian ironwood, cryptomeria, chestnut, and camellia. Posts of bamboo were also widely used. Again, the shelves adjoining the tokonoma took on new styles and employed a variety of different woods.

Sukiya techniques were also applied to windows and roofs, and it is largely because of the ingenuity of the sukiya designers that we have so many variations of these features today. It requires only a glance at the photographs in this book to understand the extent to which the sukiya style carried such variations, and it would be tedious to enumerate them here. We have already taken note of the sukiya-style treatment of windows, and we need only mention here that the traditional materials of thatch, tile, and wood or bark shingles were used for roofs. It was in the style of the roof, of course, rather than in its materials, that the sukiya designers demonstrated their special capacity for innovation.

In its refinement of the features that it adapted from the minka and the shoin styles, the sukiya style thus served as a seedbed for the development of new concepts and techniques. In contrast with the older styles, which were almost purely static, it was unmistakably dynamic, and its inspirations are just as strong today as they were in Momoyama and early Edo times. We must remind ourselves, however, that none of this would have been possible without the economic circumstances that existed in the days when the sukiya style was born—specifically, the affluence that permitted the expenditure of a great deal of time, labor, and money. Without the rise of a prosperous merchant class (which was eventually to eclipse the warrior class in financial power), the sukiya style might well have withered away soon after it appeared. Fortunately, it did quite the opposite, and in its flourishing it provided the motivation for its own creativity and the production of more and more variations of traditional forms.

10. Functional Planning

In its basic planning, the sukiya style makes use of a paper model for each room to be constructed: a three-dimensional representation which can be folded flat or set up to form the shape of the room in miniature (about one-twentieth of its actual projected size). On this *okoshi-e-zu,* as it is called, the component elements of the room are indicated—floor, walls, ceiling, fusuma, shoji, windows, and the like—as well as dimensions, colors, and textures. This method of architectural planning seems to have originated in the early Edo period, but the oldest examples of okoshi-e-zu that exist today date from the latter part of that period. Among these the finest are the ones made under the guidance of Matsudaira Rakuo (1758–1829), daimyo of Shirakawa (in the present Fukushima Prefecture), tea master, poet, and patron of the arts.

The okoshi-e-zu consists only of its six surfaces, representing the floor, the sides, and the ceiling of a room. No actual representations of the posts are included, although their placement is tentatively indicated. The reason for this is that the sukiya style, unlike the minka, calls for no fixed arrangement of posts within the total floor area. In fact, except for the strategic ones at the corners, the posts can be placed quite freely at the discretion of the sukiya designer, and sometimes they need not even stand at the corners. In the minka style, on the other hand, the majority of the posts have the function of supporting a rather large, heavy roof and are therefore arranged in a fixed pattern which cannot be changed. The sukiya style created rooms one by one, while the minka, as well as the shinden and the shoin, created rooms by dividing a large space —that is, the total framework of the building—into smaller spaces whose boundaries were fixed by the placement of the posts.

In the long history of Japanese architecture it was the sukiya style which first defined a building—whether private residence, restaurant, inn, or geisha quarters—as a collection of rooms rather than a boxlike structure divided into compartments. The okoshi-e-zu is thus symbolic not only of the teahouse and the buildings evolved from it but also of the whole concept of space and functional planning that distinguishes the sukiya style. Although none of this is new to modern architecture, it must be remembered that it was hardly less than epoch-making in Japanese architectural history.

The sukiya style, although it evolved from the minka through the medium of the teahouse, is fundamentally different from the minka style. Some of the differences have already been noted, but it will be worthwhile here to enlarge a bit on this subject. As a matter of fact, the relation of the sukiya style to the minka is something like the relation of what the Japanese call a "demon child" to his parents. He resembles neither of them, and his behavior is unruly and unpredictable.

The concept of space in the sukiya style is far different from that in the minka, and thus there is a wide difference in appearance and atmosphere. The minka begins with a basic structure and framework within which the rooms and their functions are determined. The sukiya building has no such basic structure to limit its design, nor is it inhibited by such necessities as having to accommodate its floor space to the arrangement of the posts. In the minka the posts vary considerably in thickness—from about one foot for those which provide the main support to about 4.8 and 3.9 inches for lesser ones. This in itself lends a certain air of heaviness to the minka structure. In the sukiya-style building, however, the posts are more or less of uniform thickness. Those of the Katsura villa, which are fairly typical, run to about 4.8 inches. Why, we may ask, should there be such a difference?

The answer, of course, lies in the basic framework. As in the construction of temples and shrines, there is always a basic structural pattern for the minka. The most common form of this framework in traditional Japanese architecture is the post-and-beam system, which has the function not only of supporting the roof but also of providing stability during earthquakes. In Japan, of course, this is a prime consideration. Load-bearing walls have no part in this system, not only because they tend to collapse in a strong earthquake but also because they inhibit ventilation. Since the Japanese summer is extremely hot and humid, wall areas in traditional architecture have been kept to a minimum, and an open-sided structure with removable shoji and fusuma has always been preferred. In any case, buildings which comprise a number of rooms require a fairly complicated system of posts and beams to provide stability and to support the weight of the roof. And the basic arrangement of the posts, which is predetermined and cannot be changed without inviting the collapse of the structure, naturally determines the division and functions of the enclosed space.

No floor plan for the minka-style structure can ignore the position of the posts. In most cases they serve to designate the corners of the rooms—that is, the points between which sliding partitions will be installed to divide the total floor space. No matter where they stand or how much they may spoil the appearance of the interior because of their inconvenient positions, the posts have to be dealt with, since they cannot be removed. Moreover, supplementary posts have to be added during the construction of such elements as closets and the tokonoma. These posts, however, are not required for the stability of the building itself and can therefore be smaller than those which form part of the basic system. At the same time their placement is not necessarily determined by the overall framework. Additional exterior posts are needed when a lean-to roof is built. From all of this it is easy to see why the minka style introduced posts of various sizes and why uniformity of size was out of the question. It may be further noted that in cases where the functional differentiation of space is simple and no further division into smaller rooms is necessary, as in temples and shrines, the arrangement of the posts offers far fewer problems in planning for the utilization of interior space. In the ordinary house, however, the situation is quite different.

Sukiya-style architecture is in quite another category. Here, primary attention is given to the floor plan and the functional elements. There is nothing like the basic framework of the minka style. As a matter of fact, it is only after the floor plan has been determined that consideration is given to the supporting framework. We can therefore say that in the minka style the structure restricts the floor plan, while in the sukiya style the floor plan restricts the structure. Furthermore, in the sukiya style the floor plan is determined on the basis of function. With no need to worry about the limitations imposed by a predetermined framework of posts and beams, the sukiya designer can freely decide the necessary sizes and functions of rooms, the number of rooms to be constructed, and the positions they will occupy in relation to one another. To recapitulate, the floor plan of the minka-style building represents the compartmentalization of a single unit into rooms, whereas the floor plan of the sukiya style represents an assemblage of single rooms, each of which is a unit in itself. How these units are grouped together does not matter at all.

It goes without saying that the sukiya-style room requires four corner posts, but there is no set formula for the distance between them or for the shape of the room they create, either square or rectangular. They are the major functional posts in the framework, but of course others are added. None of these supplementary posts, however, need occupy an arbitrary position. Their placement is up to the designer, and consequently the arrangement is different in every sukiya-style plan. Again, it is the placement of the posts that determines the structure and style of the roof, and here we are reminded once again that in the sukiya style the influence of the floor plan is pre-eminent. Since there is no integration of rooms under a single roof, as in the minka style, and since the arrangement of the rooms is irregular, the sukiya-style building often displays a variety of roof types and materials. In fact, the entire roof system may look most complicated, as

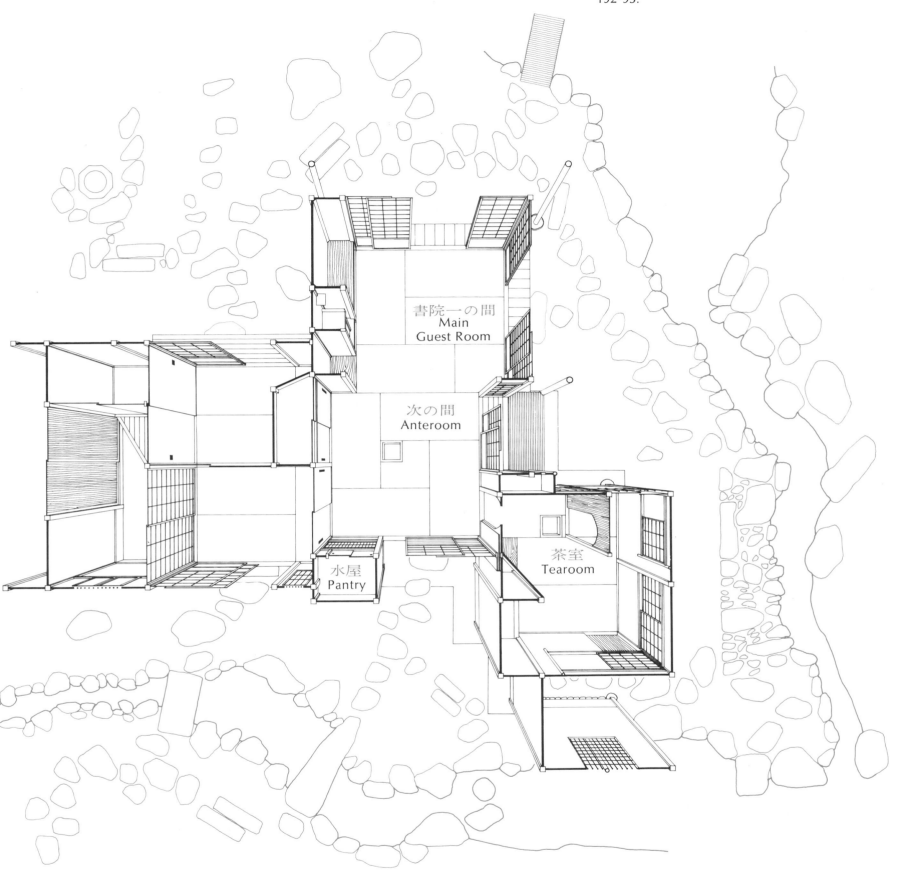

書院一の間
Main
Guest Room

次の間
Anteroom

水屋
Pantry

茶室
Tearoom

First-Floor Plan of Minoko Restaurant, Kyoto 美濃幸の一階平面図

The room just below center is a tiled bath. At left is
the garden and just above left center, the toilet.

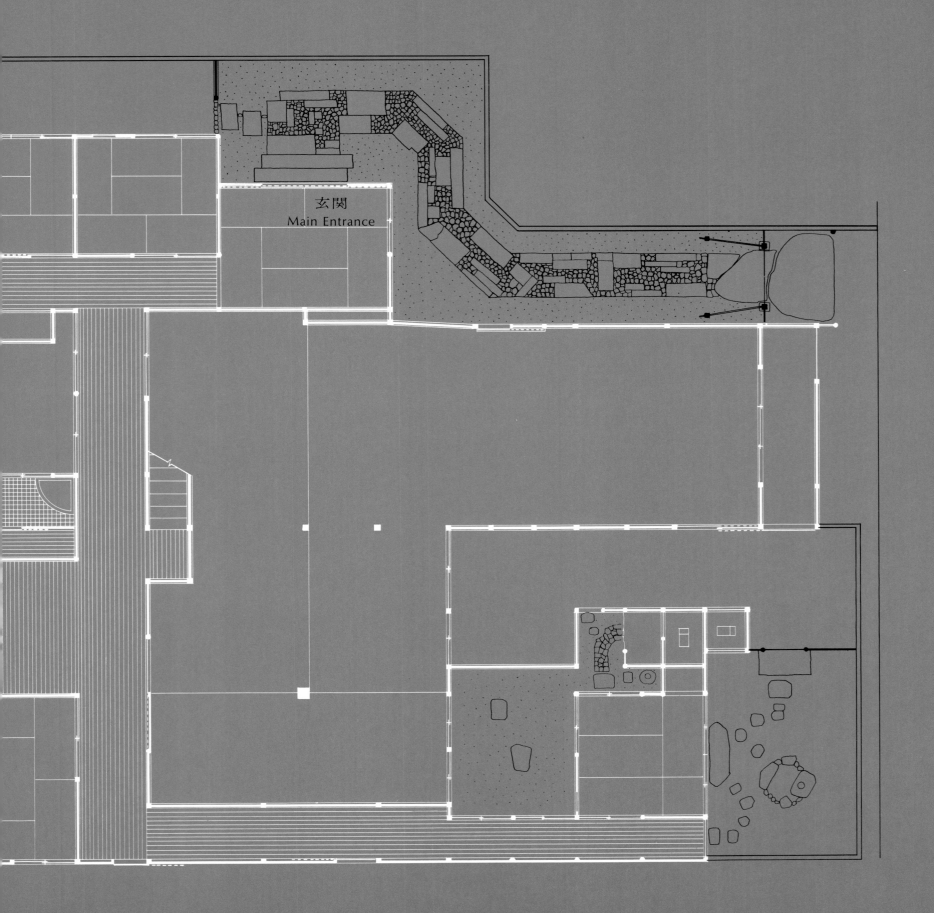

玄関
Main Entrance

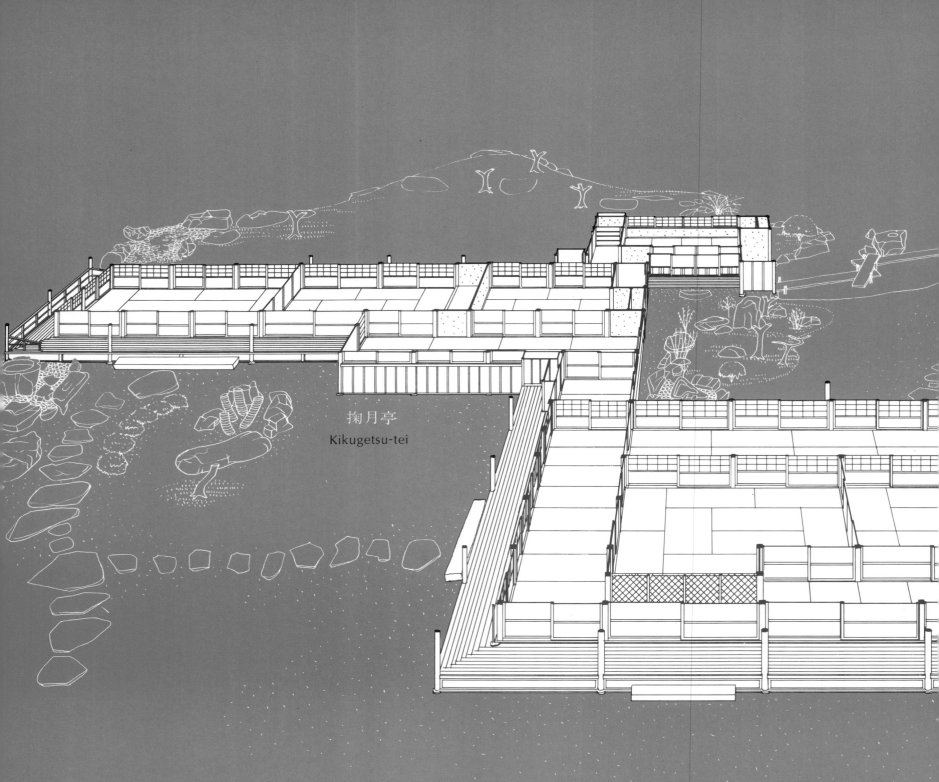

掬月亭
Kikugetsu-tei

栗林公園掬月亭北莚観の吹抜平面透視図

Plan of Kikugetsu-tei and Shoen-kan,
Ritsurin Park, Takamatsu

See photographs on pages 144-47.

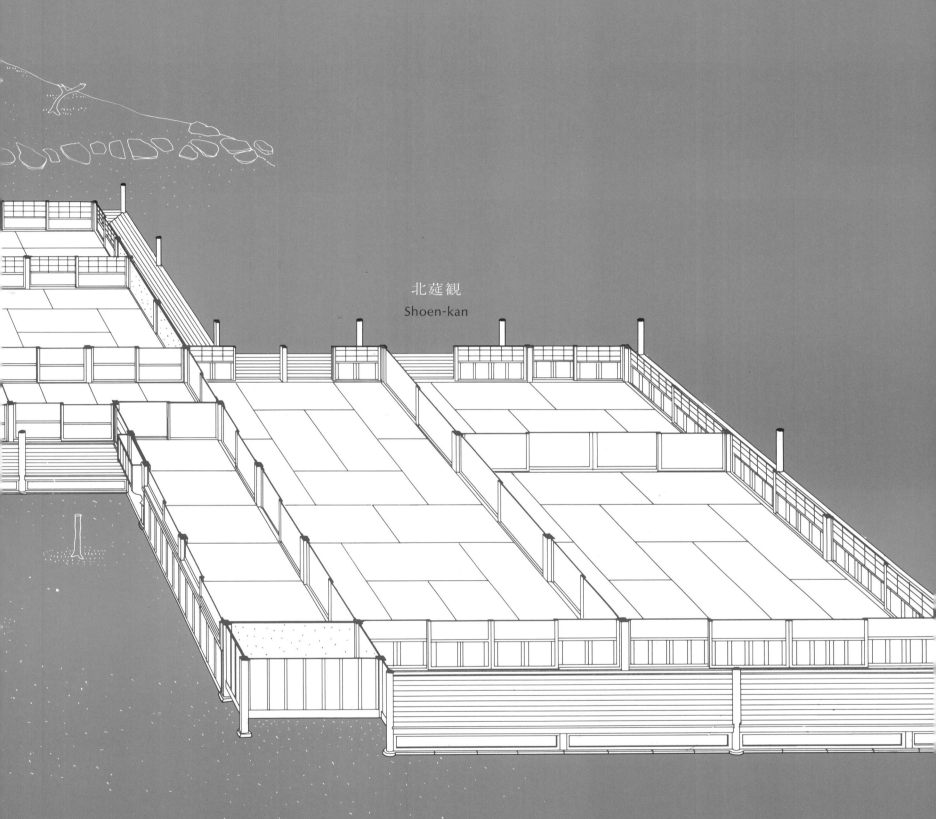

北莚観
Shoen-kan

栗林公園掬月亭北莚観の吹抜平面透視図

Plan of Kikugetsu-tei and Shoen-kan,
Ritsurin Park, Takamatsu

See photographs on pages 144-47.

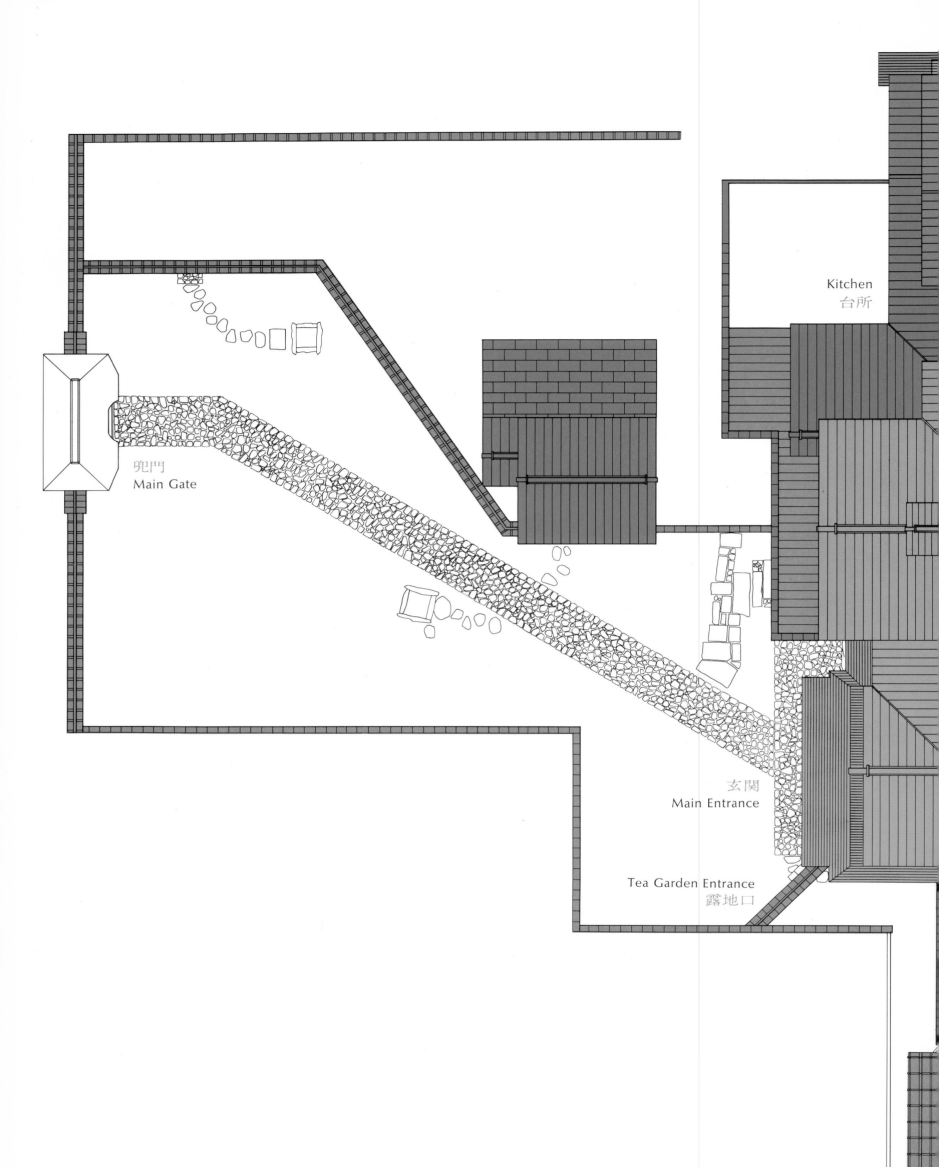

Kitchen
台所

兜門
Main Gate

玄関
Main Entrance

Tea Garden Entrance
露地口

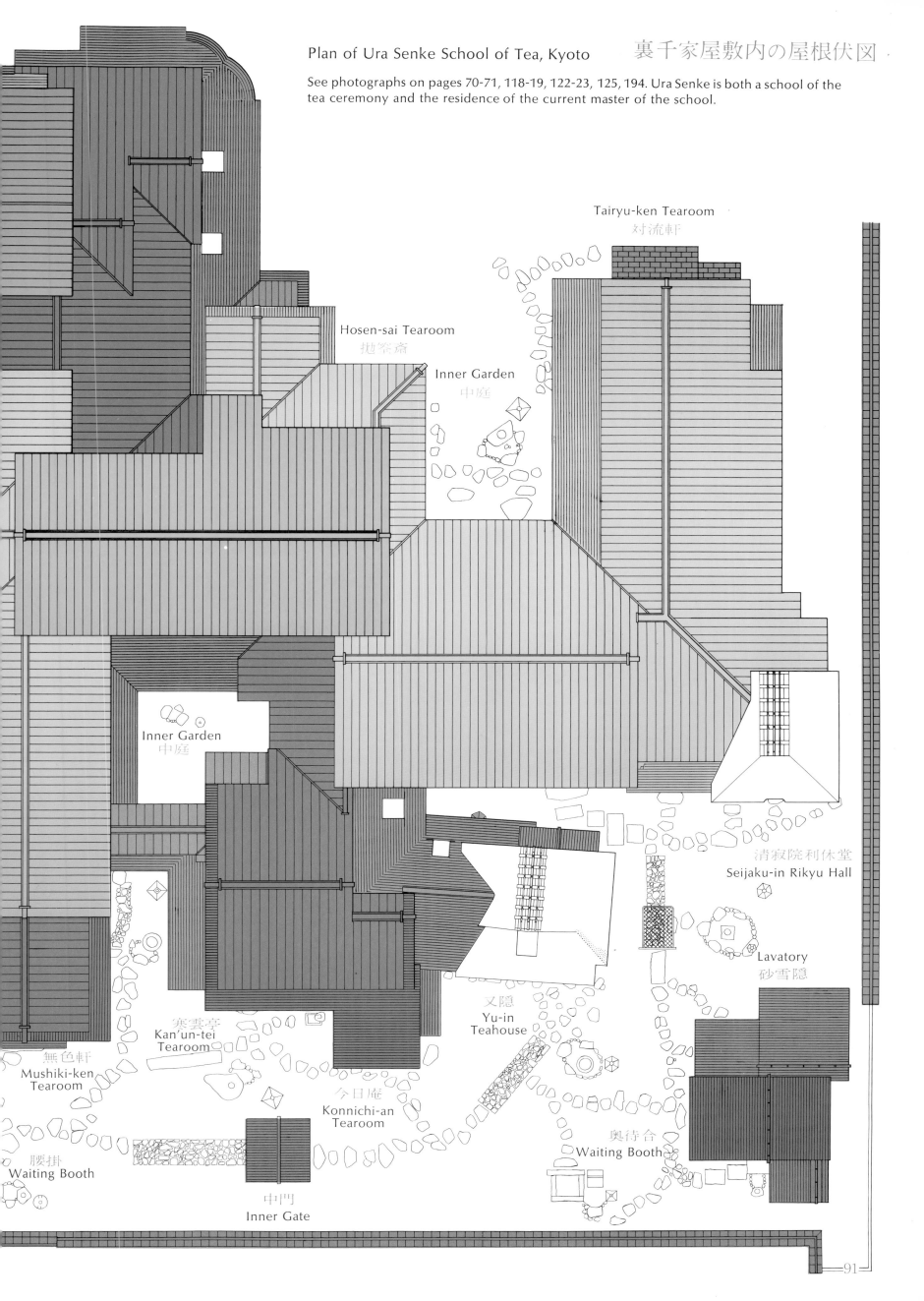

Plan of Ura Senke School of Tea, Kyoto　裏千家屋敷内の屋根伏図

See photographs on pages 70-71, 118-19, 122-23, 125, 194. Ura Senke is both a school of the tea ceremony and the residence of the current master of the school.

Tairyu-ken Tearoom
対流軒

Hosen-sai Tearoom
抛筌斎

Inner Garden
中庭

Inner Garden
中庭

清寂院利休堂
Seijaku-in Rikyu Hall

Lavatory
砂雪隠

又隠
Yu-in
Teahouse

寒雲亭
Kan'un-tei
Tearoom

無色軒
Mushiki-ken
Tearoom

今日庵
Konnichi-an
Tearoom

奥待合
Waiting Booth

腰掛
Waiting Booth

中門
Inner Gate

Plan of Kasui-en, Miyako Hotel, Kyoto

This section of the hotel (see photograph on page 93) was built in the 1950's by Togo Murano. At center is the garden.

View of inner garden, Kasui-en, Miyako Hotel, Kyoto　都ホテルの佳水園

in the Rinshun-kaku (pages 46–47) and the Katsura villa (pages 58–59). Nevertheless, the overall impression is one of extraordinary lightness in comparison with the large and heavy single-roof system of shrines, temples, and minka-style buildings. To be sure, such imposing and often massive roofs were appropriate for the buildings they covered, for they were, after all, symbols of religion or social status. But buildings in the sukiya style—villas, retreats, restaurants, inns, assignation houses, geisha quarters, and eventually the residences of commoners—had no need for such symbols and could thus express individuality in their roofs as well as in all their other features.

Since the sukiya structure consisted of a collection of rooms rather than an integration of rooms under one roof, how was it possible to achieve harmony in what at first glance gives the impression of a totally accidental grouping of disparate units? The answer, interestingly enough, is standardization, paradoxical though this may seem in the light of all that has been said about the creative originality of the sukiya style. It is not standardization, however, in the sense of such depressing modern developments as tract houses but standardization of measurements within the structure itself. This brings us back to the tatami-grid system of proportions that we have already taken note of in an earlier chapter.

In traditional Japanese architecture there are two systems of linear measurement. The first and by far the older of these, known as the post system, is based upon the distance from the center of one post to the center of the next, a fixed interval of about six feet (although this distance varies from region to region). The second, known as the tatami system and instituted in the sixteenth century, is based on the size of the tatami (roughly 6 feet by 3 feet). The post system is generally used in eastern Japan—that is, the area lying east of the Japan Alps—and the tatami system in western Japan.

Although, as we have seen, the 36-unit grid represented by a single tatami provided the sukiya designers with an excellent basis for determining proportions, the planning of a building under the tatami system was a good deal more complicated than it was under the post system. First of all, the room size depended upon the number of tatami which made up the floor area and not upon the placement of the posts. This in turn meant that the distance between the posts varied, and the work of the designer and the carpenter was thereby made more difficult than it was in the structure with a fixed system of posts. Still, the eventual standardization of the tatami size and the resulting form of mass production of tatami (and later of other elements of the building) made this work considerably easier. In any event, with the tatami as a module, it was possible to determine not only the dimensions of rooms but also those of all other elements, including corridors, shelves, closets, and the tokonoma, and thereby to attain a harmony of proportions throughout the entire sukiya structure.

The characteristics of the sukiya style naturally found expression in a wide variety of forms. Since the basic concept was a collection of rooms rather than a single building under one roof, the structure could theoretically expand forever, and the style could be applied even to large-scale construction, provided building space was available. In such massive buildings as the Great Buddha Hall of the Todai-ji temple at Nara and the Dai-goku-den of the Kyoto Imperial Palace, the builders faced the problem of constructing an enormous roof, but the expansive structure in sukiya style faces no such problem at all. Still, it is perhaps a limitation of the sukiya style that the small size of its posts precludes the construction of a building of more than two (or, at the very most, three) stories and thus forces the structure to expand horizontally rather than vertically. In urban Japan today, this is decidedly a limitation, for building space is not only at a premium but is also fantastically expensive.

In older times, when noblemen and other people of means could lavish large areas on sukiya-style construction—as at the Katsura villa, for example—rooms could expand in all directions to create interesting changes of view and dispositions of space. The surrounding terrain was of course taken into the design, and natural forms of land and water—hills, ravines, rivers, and ponds—all played a part in the planning. Needless to say, landscape gardening also played an important part in the development of the sukiya setting. Thus while the basic outline of the minka-style building remained rectangular and solid, that of the sukiya structure was capable of infinite variations and displayed great plasticity.

Yet even within a limited space—like that, for example, of an urban restaurant or inn—there are advantages in the sukiya style. Of course the space must be used to its maximum possibilities, and a garden, however small, is essential. The disposition of the individual rooms must still create a sense of openness, and rooms at the center of the construction must have good access to outdoor light. Again, if the building lot is of irregular shape, as is often the case in Japan, the sukiya style has advantages, since it adheres to no basic rectangular or square plan. Although today these factors are rather academic, since so much of Japanese architecture has turned to concrete and steel, in the feudal period they were of particular importance. In those times, when comparatively small and often irregularly shaped building lots were the only land available to commoners, construction in the sukiya style offered a most effective and excellent means of using the space to full advantage. This was one of the main reasons why the chaya—those restaurants, inns, public teahouses, and the like that we have looked at earlier—adopted the sukiya style.

Extension of the sukiya-style complex of rooms can be accomplished without destroying the beauty of the overall appearance as long as the additional construction preserves the harmony of proportion, texture, and technique. The same is true of remodeling, since there is no basic structural plan to be altered, as there would be in other architectural styles. Restaurants and inns frequently undertake such extension and remodeling, and here the sukiya style once again proves its convenience. Any extension of a shrine, a temple, or a minka-style house, however, cannot help being an architectural blemish, for it obliterates whatever beauty of shape or outline the original might have had. The amenability of the sukiya structure to extension or alteration without losing its intrinsic beauty was one of the main reasons why the sukiya style was so widely adopted for the construction of townsmen's houses during the Edo period. This was the age of the rising middle class, and its emergence into prosperity was reflected in its ability to enlarge its residences and enhance their attractiveness as its fortunes increased.

11. Colorful Presentation

One of the most interesting characteristics of the sukiya style is its fondness for the irregular floor plan. In the minka style the floor plan is basically rectangular or square (although L and U shapes also appear), and the dividing lines of the rooms usually form a grid within this basic plan. In the traditional abbot's quarters of a temple there are six rooms in two rows of three each. Similarly, the shoin style calls for a specific division of rooms within the total floor space. In the sukiya style, however, irregularity of room arrangement prevails, and no orderly system of division exists. The guest at a sukiya-style Japanese inn often has the experience of getting lost on the way from his room to the bath or the banquet hall, and the complexity of the layout may easily give him the sensation of wandering through a maze. Sometimes this intricacy may be the result of poor planning, but more frequently it is intentional. In a Western hotel one can readily find his room without the aid of a bellboy—that is, if he remembers its number—and in this sense Western hotels are more efficient, perhaps, than Japanese inns, although one can hardly say that they are more interesting.

Certainly the layout of rooms in a Japanese inn—or in any other sizable sukiya-style building—is complicated. At times we find that it has also been done with a certain sense of humor. The sedate tokonoma, for example, with its hanging scroll or its flower arrangement, may share its rear wall with the adjoining toilet, or the maids' room at an inn may be located beside the main stairway, so that the help are able to overhear what the guests have to say about the inn and its service. The rooms branch off from the twining corridors like clusters of grapes, and the guests may congratulate themselves if, after considerable wandering around, they finally arrive at the right spot without having to ask for help. But it is all part of the charm, and, as we have just noted, it is almost always intentional.

When the building area is relatively small, it is essential that the innkeeper reduce the amount of space per guest, since it is hardly conceivable that he would be willing to reduce the number of guests themselves. But it is also essential that his inn give the illusion of greater space than it actually has. Consequently, when the floor plan is intricate and the guest is never quite sure just where he is in the midst of this complex layout, he imagines the structure to be larger than it really is. The production of this psychological effect is an inherent purpose of the sukiya style, and it is exactly what sukiya designers and their clients desire in this form of architecture. It is also what the guests at a Japanese inn expect.

During our progress along a corridor in a sukiya-style building, we never quite know where we will end up. The interesting contrasts and unexpected discoveries along the way are decidedly pleasant. At the end of a narrow and rather dark hallway we may come upon a window that expands our horizon with a view of a large bright garden (page 37). Or we may pass a large banquet hall on our right and an elegant tearoom on our left. There is no end of discoveries and surprises.

The sizes of rooms at an inn may be decided quite freely according to the purpose in mind: large hall-like rooms for parties and banquets, small rooms for sleeping. No attention need be given to a restrictive floor plan, to a predetermined system of posts and beams, or to the problem of an all-embracing roof structure. The only necessity is to determine the functions of the rooms.

Generally speaking, in Western-style hotels all rooms of the same size and price have the same type of interior design. The situation in the sukiya-style inn is quite different. Even if there are five 8-tatami rooms, for example, not one of them will resemble another in atmosphere and appearance. This diversity of interior design is of course a

Interior of Ko Shoin (Old Shoin), Katsura villa, Kyoto 桂離宮　古書院の内部

reflection of the whole history of the sukiya style, which, as we have frequently noted before, developed through the employment of a variety of techniques. Naturally, a process of trial and error was involved, but the goal was always clear: originality of design and rejection of rigid formulas and stale repetition. This pursuit of variety is well illustrated in the rooms of the sukiya-style inn and particularly in the structure and design of the tokonoma. If one room, for instance, has a tokonoma with a raised tatami floor, another may have one with a board floor at the same level as the tatami floor of the room itself. If one tokonoma has its post at the corner, another may have its post set somewhat inside its outer edge. The variety of tokonoma posts has already been mentioned, and we may add that a similar variety is seen in the tokonoma framework. The same is true of the shelves that adjoin the tokonoma and of practically all the other elements of the room. Even the tape which binds the edges of the tatami may vary in color and pattern.

It will be well to take time here for a closer look at the tokonoma and its role in Japanese décor. We have already noted that it serves for the display of art objects and flower arrangements and that the most honored guest is seated in front of it—to be exact, in front of its main post. We have noted also that nothing in the line of lavish display is permissible—at most a hanging scroll and a single other objet d'art or a hanging scroll and a comparatively simple flower arrangement. The display is essentially seasonal (an appropriately symbolic scroll and an arrangement of pine, bamboo, and plum blossoms for New Year's, a scroll painting of maple leaves and an arrangement of chrysanthemums for autumn), but it must also reflect the specific occasion and the tastes of both host and guest. It goes without saying that all this requires careful thought and that it has much to do with determining the atmosphere of the room and influencing the mood of the guests. At the same time it is a reflection of sincere hospitality on the part of the host and a means of creating harmony between him and the people he is entertaining. One hardly need wonder, then, that Japanese architecture has regarded the tokonoma with a certain reverence.

The treatment of ceilings is no less various than that of the tokonoma, and here the colors and textures of wood, bamboo, and other materials are used to maximum effect in a wide range of patterns. Similarly, variety is introduced in the colors and designs of fusuma and the styles of shoji and transoms. In the shoji, for example, the pattern of the grid over which the translucent paper is pasted may be varied according to the placement of the vertical and horizontal wooden strips.

So far, we have been looking only at the interior of the room and the variations of style and treatment that give it individuality. But the outdoor scenery is also a part of the atmosphere of the room, and not merely in the picture-window sense of Western architecture. In the sukiya style the outdoor scenery is neither excluded nor considered as separate from the house. On the contrary, it is invited in, so to speak, or viewed as an extension of the room itself. And as the scenery changes from hour to hour with the changing light, and from season to season, the atmosphere of the room changes with it. The same scene may be enjoyed in different ways, according to whether the shoji are wide open, as in the more temperate months of the year, or partly closed, as in the instance of the previously described yukimi shoji. Sometimes the garden is filled with the strong and brilliant sunlight of midsummer, sometimes with the softer light of an afternoon in late autumn. Misty mornings and rainy evenings bring other changes of scene, and snowy days add a dramatic touch to this union of interior and exterior.

So it happens that we may be surprised and pleased not only by the differing designs and décor of the rooms in a sukiya-style building but also by their differing appearance in various seasons or at various hours of the day. This is the reason why we always experience a feeling of newness when we visit such rooms on different occasions. The surprise is hardly dramatic, for the essential elements do not change, but it is a pleasant one nevertheless. At the same time it is not the purpose of these rooms to overwhelm us with their attractions and thereby minimize our own importance. (Undoubtedly all of us have had the experience of rooms that do quite the opposite.) They could hardly give us pleasure, in any event, by insisting on their own superiority at the cost of our comfort. Actually their beauty is undeniable, but it serves as a setting to enhance the importance of those who use them and not as a means of brilliant architectural and decorative display.

The colors are those of nature in its more subdued moods. Although the most careful treatment is given to texture and detail, its only purpose is to bring out the natural beauty of the materials themselves. In this sense the sukiya style idealizes the beauty of nature, and it is this intention that lies at the heart of most traditional Japanese arts and crafts. We may note it particularly in the art of flower arrangement, but we find it in pottery and painting as well. The sukiya atmosphere is delicate and elegant but not exciting. No striking colors are used. For those who expect something strong and sharply stimulating, the sukiya style is often a disappointment.

Aside from its purely aesthetic values, the sukiya style has a number of practical advantages. Restaurants built in this style are able to attract customers by offering a variety of settings, so that, no matter how often one might go there, he will at least not become bored by the atmosphere. Inns enjoy the same advantage, although here there is a restriction, since there are always members of a tour party who complain that their rooms, even though the price is the same, are less attractive than those assigned to other members of the party. In contrast with villas and private residences in the sukiya style, restaurants and inns are public places, and they may be used for a number of events. Anyone may make use of the facilities as long as he is able to pay. As a result, these establishments are often used for tea-ceremony performances and flower-arrangement exhibitions. Although the cost might be prohibitive for one person alone, it is not so when it is shared by a group of people. Since a reasonably large sukiya-style establishment has a number of types of rooms (and therefore a variety of tokonoma) suitable for tea-ceremony use, students who make use of them have a greater freedom of selection than they have in their teachers' residences and can thus enlarge their knowledge of proper settings for the art of the tea ceremony and the art of flower arrangement as well.

On such occasions, office girls who study these arts and who ordinarily wear Western-style clothes can don their kimono and create the correct traditional atmosphere. Like the daughters of Edo-period townsmen, they can practice traditional etiquette as they make use of the various rooms and settings. Their topics of conversation may be modern, but much of what they discuss will turn on the aesthetics of the art they are studying. Sometimes poetry is recited, or again there may be a good deal of criticism of one another's manners and style of dress. In a certain sense they are on stage in these sukiya-style rooms, and the environment is an excellent one for displaying their sense of refinement as well as their achievements in the arts that are considered essential for the well-educated and cultured Japanese woman.

Although it is doubtful that sukiya-style restaurants and inns have much influence on the design of residential architecture today, they once played an important role in this respect. During the Edo period, whenever people found attractive designing in these places, they applied it in their own houses. In those days, of course, they could not copy the designs or techniques of the daimyo or samurai residence without grave risk of being punished for their presumption. There was no such risk, however, in copying designs used in the sukiya style. The tendency to copy the designs of sukiya-style restaurants and inns survived to a certain extent after the Meiji Restoration of 1868, when Japan's modern period began. In fact, it was still apparent up to the days of World War II, and we may even find isolated instances of it today. It was this penchant for imitation that caused some of the prewar villas of wealthy merchants to resemble high-class restaurants and inns in their general construction and the details of their design. Even now, for example, we may find instances of the use of black pebbles from the Kamo River in Kyoto or beautifully grained slabs from a tree trunk to pave a passageway. Both of these devices were first introduced in sukiya-style restaurants and inns. In earlier times, sukiya-style buildings which were open for public use were decidedly the most important models for the residential architecture of the prosperous middle class.

12. Modern Limitations

Today the sukiya style has been forced to show its limitations, particularly in urban architecture. In the past, as we have seen, one of its virtues was its ability to make efficient use of limited building space. At present, although urban building space is more limited than ever, new architectural techniques and methods of construction are even more capable of using limited space to best advantage. As long as these modern techniques remained more or less isolated from the general current of Japanese architecture and were confined to such downtown structures as office buildings and Western-style hotels, the sukiya style could maintain its existence, but now modern architecture has permeated the length and breadth of Japan, and its techniques are readily available to anyone who wishes to use them. Naturally, economic considerations are a part of this, and it must be admitted that the sukiya style is an expensive one.

To begin with, since the cost of urban land is outrageously high, it has become an extravagance to build in the sukiya style, which at best can permit a building of two or three stories. Small plots of land like those that once served as seedbeds for the sukiya style are now integrated in order to provide building space for much larger and more economical structures. Wood, which was once pre-eminent among building materials, has now been replaced by concrete and steel. There seems to be no recourse for the sukiya style but to surrender the stage completely or to retire from the cities to the countryside.

In its dependence on wood the sukiya style suffers from still another modern limitation. It has been suggested that concrete and steel could be substituted for wood, at

京都の町並み

least externally, in sukiya-style construction. This suggestion need not be considered sacrilegious, for it was sincerely made in the interest of preserving the style in the face of increasing competition from modern architecture, but to the genuine admirer of the style it is sacrilegious nonetheless. The essence of sukiya architecture is wood, and without wood there would no longer be a sukiya style. To be sure, wood is highly inflammable, and this is practically a fatal deficiency in the crowded cities of Japan today. It was an even more fatal deficiency in feudal times, when devastating fires were almost a commonplace in Japanese cities, but of course this did not deter the sukiya designers, since it was inconceivable to use any other material, even if it had been available. Although wood can be treated chemically to make it fireproof, such treatment only destroys the natural beauty that the sukiya style seeks to emphasize. Thus the question of using anything but natural wood is at best academic.

Since wood is unsuitable for tall buildings, and particularly since the posts in sukiya-style architecture are necessarily slender, there is also no question of building to greater heights and thereby assuring more economic use of the building space. For purposes of safety and fire prevention, Japanese building regulations restrict the height of the sukiya structure to three stories, even though two stories is almost always the limit in actual practice. In any case, considering the ever increasing demand for land to build apartment houses and office buildings—to say nothing of freeways and public parks—it is unprofitable to construct buildings of such limited height. Consequently, even if a sukiya-style building is constructed in the midst of the city, it will not only represent a fearful extravagance but will also quickly come to have a shabby look because of air pollution and the general filth that is characteristic of the modern metropolis.

The sukiya style suffers from yet other modern limitations. Or perhaps we should say that it suffers from the conditions of modern life. Buildings of concrete and steel are built to resist all manner of shocks, but the sukiya-style building is fragile indeed in the presence of heavy traffic in the streets and the machinery of modern domestic life. A wooden house in sukiya style can easily be twisted out of shape by the repeated tremors caused by passing trucks and trains or even by the vibrations of such household conveniences as electric refrigerators and washing machines. Not only these, however, but also air conditioning and central heating are ruinous to such a house, since the great difference between outdoor and indoor temperatures causes the wood to dry out and warp. Naturally, since the sukiya style was not created in the machine age, it never conceived of such problems. Nor have these problems been satisfactorily solved by modern sukiya designers.

No less inimical to the existence of the sukiya style today is the lack of specially trained craftsmen. In fact, the quality of carpentry has so declined today that even farmers who come to the cities for work during the slack season at home are able to fill most of the requirements. It might even be said that today's carpenters are no longer craftsmen but laborers. Although a carpenter of small skill might be able to build a house in sukiya style by following basic instructions, it is almost certain that such a house would look decidedly unrefined in comparison with the masterpieces of true sukiya craftsmen.

This is by no means the end of the problems. The cost of the sukiya-style building itself is extremely high. Since such architecture calls for the use of select materials and highly skilled labor, only the most affluent of Japanese can afford it. Carpenters, provided skilled ones can be found, may spend only half a day on the actual construction and the other half on the care of their tools. The use of electric saws and planes is excluded, since they cannot produce the effects desired. Inevitably the work must be done by hand if the natural beauty of the wood is to be stressed. Quite often, in fact, the cost per square foot of construction is approximately $50. When we consider that the figure for a modern office building is only about half this amount, it is easy to see that the expense is prohibitive. Moreover, since there is no prospect that the cost of labor and materials will ever decrease, the unit cost of sukiya-style construction can do nothing but go up.

It may well be that the sukiya style is on its way to extinction. If it has already accomplished its historical mission and its social functions and is about to leave the stage, it would seem useless to try to hold it back for sentimental reasons, let us say, or for the purpose of preserving a part of architectural history intact. Today, more rapidly than ever, values are undergoing reconversion, and old ones are often cast aside. The conditions that produced and sustained the sukiya style for the long stretch of more than three centuries have all but disappeared, and present conditions do not favor its survival. Modern architecture is forced to look toward the future; it cannot concern itself with the preservation of the past, even though what it learns from the past is often highly profitable. The requirements of today and tomorrow are for high-quality construction which can be accomplished with speed and without the necessity of superior craftsmen like those demanded by the sukiya style. Indeed, in the presence of modern architecture, the sukiya style might almost be said to have an absurd look,

◀ Aerial view of central Kyoto

not only because it represents an age long past but also because it represents a hardly less than ridiculous extravagance.

In spite of all this, the Japanese have a deep affection for this now largely outmoded and yet elegantly beautiful style. Although we cannot ignore the role that tradition plays in this affection—that is, a sentimental admiration for the old simply because it is old—we are still forced to admit that the style is beautiful in its own right. And it is for this reason that Japanese architecture today, despite its modernization, often manages to incorporate elements of the sukiya style. One example is to be found in the shops that occupy the basements or ground floors of the newest and most up-to-date buildings. Quite frequently, such shops employ traditional sukiya techniques, although of course on a much smaller scale. One thinks, for example, of a tempura restaurant in the basement of one of Tokyo's latest office buildings, where one steps from an ultramodern corridor into a pleasant adaptation from the past—not strictly old-fashioned, to be sure, and certainly not utterly faithful to the style, but decidedly refreshing nonetheless. It does not matter that the style is not always correctly interpreted. The important thing is that it has been taken into this modern structure and has thus been able to survive, even in what might be called a hostile environment. There is evidence here not only that the Japanese have an innate fondness for the sukiya style but also that they have been trained, so to speak, to the sukiya manner. Where the style is appropriate, it is still maintained, partly because of its long tradition but largely because of its own attractions.

Occasionally also, in large modern buildings, one finds a room designed in the sukiya style and set aside for use by employees who are studying the tea ceremony, flower arrangement, or the chanting of texts from the Noh drama. Activities like these, sponsored at company expense, are part of the after-hours cultural programs that many large Japanese firms offer their workers. Usually the room provided for such activities follows quite closely the sukiya style of the past, although here, as in the above-mentioned shops, it is only part of an alien interior and not an independent structure like the sukiya buildings of earlier times.

Perhaps it is through such adaptations as these—through incorporation into the interior design of modern architecture—that the sukiya style can best be preserved. Here, at least, it can be free from the earth-shaking traffic and unclean air that threaten the existence of the independent sukiya structure. Admittedly there is a certain sadness in this kind of survival, but there is also the consolation that an excellent philosophy of design has not been thoughtlessly cast aside.

13. Modern Trends

It was inevitable that the sukiya style should be affected by the great influx of Western styles of architecture that began with the advent of Japan's modern age in 1868. At first, however, the Western influence was limited to the larger cities and to public buildings. While it is true that a number of government officials and prosperous businessmen built Western-style houses, there was actually no threat to the sukiya style for another half century or so. In fact, even though prominent persons might build their official residences in Western style, it was still the sukiya style that they preferred for their private villas. At the same time, although Western-style restaurants began to appear in the cities, there were actually not many of them, and their limited and rather uninspired menus did not attract large numbers of customers. Consequently there was little threat to the traditional sukiya-style restaurant until a drastic change in Japanese eating habits occurred, and this actually did not take place until after the Pacific War.

Nevertheless, the sukiya style could not close its eyes to the modernist ideology of Western architecture that began to pervade Japan during the Taisho era (1912–26). Rather than say, however, that it viewed this trend as a threat to its own existence, it would be better to say that it was surprised to discover the many ways in which its concepts of design resembled those of the new architecture. For this reason it took advantage of the trend to reassess and modernize its own ideas.

There was a decided difference between the Western world and Japan in their absorption of modern architectural ideology. While Occidentals in general accepted it by turning away from tradition and bidding farewell to the past, the Japanese found in it a means for carrying on their traditions in new forms. Even as late as the 1930's, architectural journalism in Japan was emphasizing the resemblances between traditional Japanese architecture and the modern architecture of the West, thereby giving clear evidence of unwillingness to turn aside from the past. At the same time, however, the impact of ideas from the West had the effect of curing the nationalism and isolationism that had characterized Japanese architecture before.

One of the men who contributed greatly to the sensitive modernization of the sukiya style is still among the foremost of Japan's architectural designers. He is Isoya Yoshida, who was born in 1894. Two years after graduating from the Tokyo University of Arts,

Miyuki Room, Hassho-kan restaurant, Nagoya　八勝館　御幸の間の内部

he went to Europe to study the new style of architecture in Germany. To his regret, he discovered a good deal less to admire in it than he had expected. On the other hand he was much impressed by the Renaissance and Gothic styles, even though he realized their complete unsuitability to Japan and the Japanese, no matter how appropriate they were in Europe. Recognizing what he felt to be an almost fatal difference of nationalist ideologies in architecture, he decided not to pursue Western concepts at all but instead to create something authentically Japanese in which the West could find a model. As the basis for modernizing Japanese architecture and relating it more closely to the needs of contemporary life, he chose the traditional sukiya style. Beginning with the private residence of Nobuko Yoshiya, a well-known woman novelist, he experimented with a number of techniques and within a short time developed a style of his own.

One of his innovations was the *o-kabe* style of wall, in which the posts were exposed on the interior side only. Heretofore the sukiya style had largely employed the *shin-kabe* wall, which exposed the posts on both sides but did not meet with new urban building regulations requiring completely plastered exterior walls as a means of fire prevention. Although there already existed a style of wall in which the posts were visible on the inside only, the effect it produced was quite heavy, and Yoshida's new version was much lighter in comparison. It also had the virtue of permitting a more irregular and therefore more free arrangement of posts, since they were no longer visible from the outside. Thus, through this regeneration of a traditional style of wall construction, Yoshida opened the way for many beautiful variations.

Taking note of the changes in architectural taste that were becoming increasingly evident in Japan, he found that modern-minded people considered traditional sukiya architecture to be too much concerned with delicate detail. Consequently he undertook other innovations. He eliminated the transom and left the space quite frankly open. In place of the former hanging struts that suspended the lintels he inserted steel dowels. For the ceiling he used unusually large sheets of wood—even up to the tatami size of 3 by 6 feet—an innovation that was difficult to achieve at that time, since such material was far less readily available than it is today. The effect of such a ceiling was much more casual and carefree than that of the traditional sukiya-style ceiling. Another of his original ideas, the use of an irregular grid for the shoji, has been much copied in present-day Japanese architecture. In all of these respects he infused the sukiya style with a sense of modern design.

Going even further, he omitted some of the corner posts, substituting others to support the weight of the roof and thereby providing the opportunity to create larger open spaces when fusuma and shoji were removed. Again, taking account of the fact that chairs had arrived on the scene to compete with the traditional sitting cushions, he introduced the concept of varying floor levels: a lower level for the section of a room in which chairs would be used, a higher level for the tatami section with sitting cushions. His purpose here was to permit the coexistence of two customs in a harmonious arrangement.

It is said that Yoshida developed his design concepts through a process of subtraction and addition—that is, by subtracting from the sukiya style those elements that were unsuitable to modern living and by adding to it a number of new materials and techniques. Whatever his method, he was the only architect who applied new techniques to the sukiya style during the period before the Pacific War. Today these techniques have come into common use. Certainly if the sukiya style requires creative originality and genuine artistry in its designers, Yoshida fills the requirement to perfection.

We have noted that modern architecture found a surprising number of its concepts reflected in the traditional sukiya style. It will be of interest in this connection to observe the reactions of a Western architect who made this discovery some three decades ago. In 1933, when Bruno Taut came to Japan as an exile from Nazi Germany, he began his study of Japanese architecture. It was the Katsura villa that inspired his greatest admiration, for he found in it a reflection of his own modernist concepts. On the other hand the Ninomaru halls of Nijo Castle held no attraction for him, even though their arrangement closely resembles that of the buildings at Katsura. Both of these structures answer certain of the requirements of modernism, including standardization of material and the use of modular design. But neither Taut nor any other modern architect could find true value in the Ninomaru halls, for their elaborately sculptured woodwork and their gorgeous wall and fusuma paintings are altogether alien to the modern concept of strictly limited decoration. It is the simplicity of Katsura that commands the modernist's admiration—this, and its emphasis on the natural beauty of its materials in posts, beams, ceilings, and walls.

Of no less interest to Taut and other modern architects from the West was the discovery that the sukiya style, in the functional arrangement of its rooms, expressed their own ideas of the proper use of space—specifically, by allowing easy access to the various areas of the structure and obviating the necessity of wasteful movement by those who used it. As a collection of rooms rather than an arbitrary compartmentalization of space within a boxlike structure, the sukiya building displayed the flexibility that modernism demanded.

Since the sukiya style already embodied elements of modernism, Japanese architects, unlike many of their counterparts in the West, could accept the new ideology without any feeling of resistance and without psychological complications. In fact, when we look at certain modern structures in Japan, it is often difficult to tell whether they were constructed according to purely Western concepts or whether they reflect elements of the sukiya style. In any case there is no point in attempting to make such an analysis, and no one in Japan has ever thought of doing so.

What is important is that the ideology of modern architecture found easy acceptance in Japan. Whether this was good or not, we cannot judge at present, although it must be admitted that at times the modern style was interpreted in the Japanese manner without a true understanding of its principles. Certainly the new ideology contributed to the modernization of Japanese architectural thought.

At the same time it is astonishing that there was no real struggle against it. This phenomenon of accepting the new without resistance could of course be observed in the early Meiji era, but it often represented a surrender of integrity and a denial of human values. For Western architects, when their ideology was not accepted either socially or politically, there were usually only three choices: to be punished by a harsh government, as under the Nazi dictatorship (in extreme cases even by death), to go into exile, or to remain silent. In Japan, to be sure, Sen no Rikyu and Furuta Oribe were also punished by a military dictatorship for insisting on their ideology and were forced to take their own lives. But this was in feudal times, and no such extreme measures were taken against the proponents of modernism in the present century. No doubt the chief reason for their immunity was that functionalism had become more and more the keynote in Japanese architecture and in Japanese society as well. Moreover, the adaptation of the sukiya style to modern demands did not constitute a sudden and complete break with tradition. Nor did the newly evolving style of modern architecture come into conflict with the demands of the ruling class. In effect, there was an adjustment between the two, and the traditional Japanese philosophy of adaptation to the flow of time and circumstances once again prevailed.

In view of the relative ease with which this accommodation was made, it may be well to summarize here the achievements of the sukiya style that particularly enabled it to play a role in the transition to modern styles. In the first place, it began as a strongly individualistic style and was, as we have seen, the only style of Japanese architecture that developed a nomenclature based on the names of its designers—that is, the konomi which has been discussed in an earlier chapter. In the second place, the sukiya is the only style in the history of Japanese architecture that transcended the boundaries of social class, for it was applied to the houses of townsmen and the villas of the aristocracy alike and to such public buildings as restaurants and inns. In the third place, the sukiya-style building, both in its harmony of structure and in its emphasis on the natural beauty of its materials, originated a code of values that endures even today.

There is another point of interest that deserves mention here. The organic materials of the traditional sukiya style, such as wood, clay, and bamboo, have the quality of controlling the atmospheric conditions within the building—that is, when central heating and air conditioning are not part of the environment. A building made of such inorganic materials as concrete, plastic, and steel does not display this quality. Since the ability of wood and clay to absorb moisture is much higher than that of materials like concrete, the interior surfaces of the sukiya-style room never give a feeling of wetness even in extremely humid weather. It is also true that a building made of organic materials is cooler in summer and warmer in winter. While such considerations may seem rather academic in a day when space heaters and air conditioners are no longer luxuries in Japan, it should be remembered that such conveniences are by no means in universal use. Nor are they necessarily preferred by all Japanese. In any event it is worth noting that the wooden house has decidedly not been supplanted by the house built of synthetics and that it still offers an environment for comfortable and, one might say, natural living. This fact alone suggests that our modern age can still find values in the sukiya style.

Nevertheless, we are not living in the past, and it is impossible today for the sukiya style to maintain the prestige it once enjoyed in the history of Japanese architecture. Modern conditions are in general inimical to its survival, but certainly its concepts of design are far from being antiquated by the ideology of modernism. In fact, as we have observed more than once before, modern architecture has not only embraced its concepts but has also undertaken to carry them forward into new realms of achievement.

PART THREE
High-lights of the Sukiya Style

1. The Diagonal-Line Approach

Although the main gate of a temple or a shrine or any similar monumental structure stands on a straight line with the main hall, that of the sukiya structure is almost invariably placed on a diagonal line in relation to the main entrance of the building itself. We have already taken note of this diagonal-line approach, but it deserves somewhat more attention here, since it is an important characteristic of the sukiya style. In Japanese it is known as *sumi-chigai* or *suji-chigai,* and these words apply to the sukiya-style floor plan as well.

The concept of slantwise rather than straight-line arrangement originated in the tea ceremony and is expressed in many aspects of this art. In the tea garden, for example, where guests stop at a stone water basin for a ceremonial rinsing of their hands before entering the teahouse, the wooden dipper is never laid straight across the basin but always on a slant. In the tearoom itself the utensils are similarly placed in diagonal relationships to one another. Kobori Enshu, whose ideas of sukiya design we have noted previously, was especially fond of such slantwise arrangements, and we can observe in his book on the tea ceremony that he paid great attention to the effective placement of the tea caddy, the dipper, the tea bowls, and other paraphernalia of the ritual. Naturally, he also applied the principle of diagonal arrangement to his architectural and garden designs.

In borrowing this principle from the tea ceremony, the sukiya style rejected the monotony of purely symmetrical arrangement and thereby added what we may call the element of pleasant surprise, both in the structure itself and in its setting. There are no head-on views and direct presentations. One does not see the main entrance from the gate, nor do the rooms stand in predictable sequence or foursquare order. The gate may be at the right or left front or even at the side but not directly ahead of the main entrance to the building. One approaches indirectly, and the revelation of the building is gradual rather than immediate.

To be precise, there are three traditional lines of approach. The first of these is the pure diagonal, which is exemplified in the approach from the inner gate to the entrance porch of the shoin at the Katsura villa (pages 112–13, right of center at top). After crossing an earthen bridge (see plan on pages 114–15), the visitor stands at the thatch-roofed inner gate. What he sees straight ahead of him is the lattice window and the veranda called Tora-en (Tiger Veranda), which are both adjacent to the porch, but not the porch itself, which comprises the official entrance. As he passes through the inner gate, he finds himself on a path paved with closely placed irregular sections of stone in a mosaic arrangement. This type of diagonal approach is used repeatedly at Katsura, sometimes as pavement, sometimes as steppingstones. It is also frequently found at restaurants and inns—for example, at the Ichiriki-tei in Kyoto. The functional advantage of such an approach is that it gives an impression of greater space than actually exists. Even if the distance between gate and entrance is quite short, it appears to be longer and therefore more interesting, and the building itself is not straightforwardly and prosaically revealed.

The second type of approach is L-shaped rather than purely diagonal, so that the path from the gate makes either a right- or a left-hand turn between the gate and the main entrance to the building. Here again, even though the building lot may be quite small, a longer approach can be obtained, and thus the impression of a larger area is given. Since it is almost impossible to see the entrance from the gate, there is once again the pleasure of suspense and curiosity, as well as that of changing scenery, as one progresses along the path. Perhaps the best example of the L-shaped approach is to be found at the Sumiya, a well-known ageya (a house where geisha entertain their customers) in the Shimabara district of Kyoto. In this case, what the visitor sees directly ahead of him from the gate is the entrance to the kitchen. This alone might well give him a sense of narrowness and confinement, but the approach now turns directly to the right and gives him a feeling of expanding space as he moves toward the main entrance. Although the approach is of course a single unit of space, the turning point serves as a border between the outer public world and the world of private pleasure and thereby induces a change of mood and consciousness in the customers. The humdrum outside world is left behind as they emerge into the world of entertainment. Needless to say, this is a clever way to attract more people into the never-never land of gaiety and delightful relaxation.

The third style among traditional approaches is not actually diagonal but curved and is probably best exemplified in that of the Omote Senke school of tea in Kyoto (pages 120–21, 126–27). This style is usually employed when there is a comparatively large area between the gate and the main entrance. At Omote Senke the approach is a paved walk bordered with graveled areas and screens of shrubbery clipped to resemble walls. The curved approach, like the pure diagonal and the L-shaped approaches, does not permit a full view of the main entrance from the gate. In fact, the main entrance is often not visible at all and only begins to reveal itself in a series of changing views as one nears the building. Again, like the other two, the curved style of approach is designed with careful consideration for the sequence of spatial experience, as we may call it, and for a corresponding sequence of emotional reactions to scenery and structure as one moves from gate to main entrance.

Aerial view of Katsura
villa and garden, Kyoto

桂離宮　書院の俯瞰

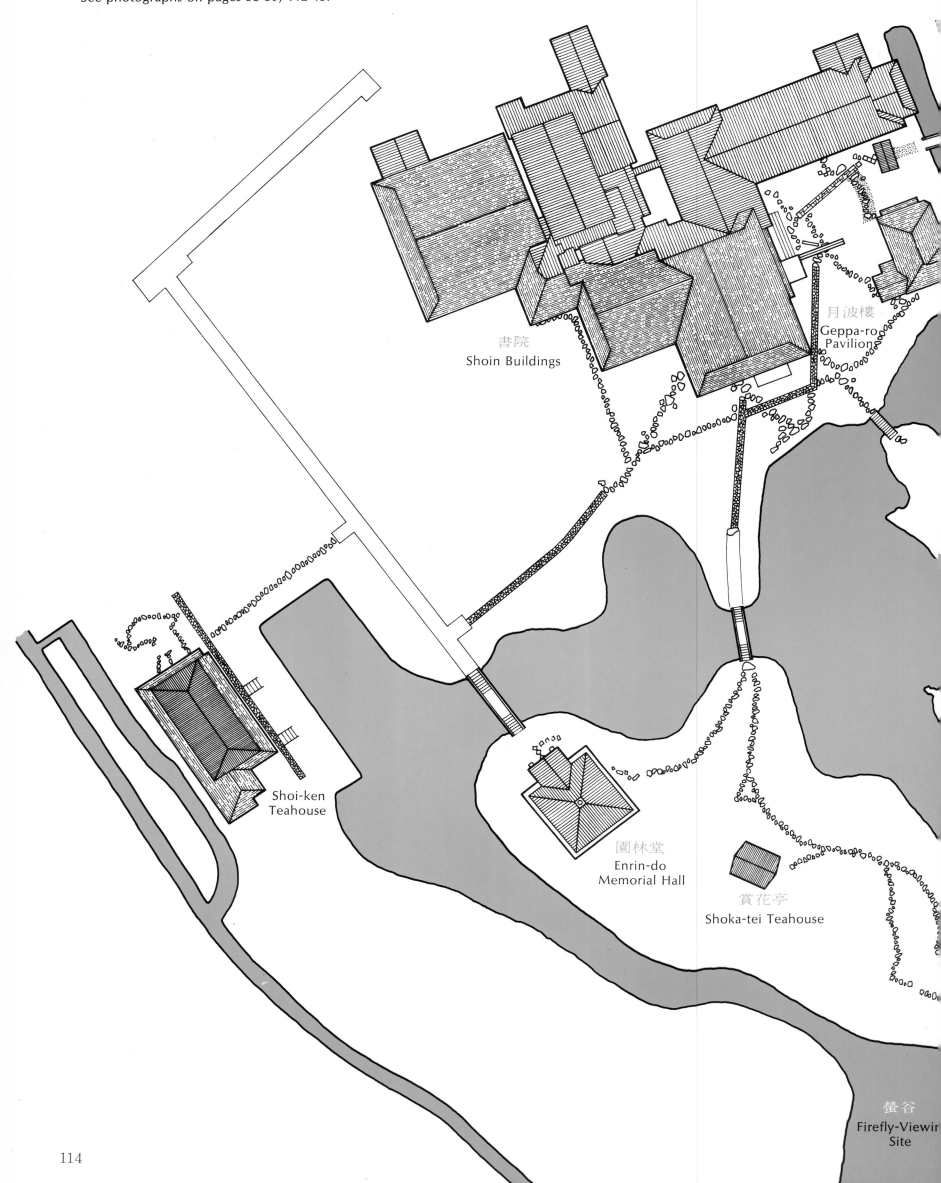

桂離宮の苑路およびアプローチ図

Plan of Katsura Villa and Garden, Kyoto

See photographs on pages 58-59, 112-13.

書院
Shoin Buildings

月波樓
Geppa-ro Pavilion

Shoi-ken Teahouse

園林堂
Enrin-do Memorial Hall

賞花亭
Shoka-tei Teahouse

螢谷
Firefly-Viewing Site

御舟屋
Boathouse

Imperial Gate
御幸門

Waiting Booth
外腰掛

Shokin-tei
Teahouse
松琴亭

Manji-tei
Teahouse
卍亭

...tral
...nd

115

Approach to Fushin-an teahouse, Omote Senke school of tea, Kyoto

Steppingstones and stone steps, Katsura villa, Kyoto　　左—表千家　不審庵へのアプローチ　　右—桂離宮　書院御輿寄前の石段

Garden paths, Ura
Senke school of tea,
Kyoto

裏千家　庭内の延段

◀ Approach to main entrance, Omote Senke school of tea, Kyoto

Approach to Ura Senke school of tea, Kyoto

Main entrance, Ura Senke school of tea, Kyoto　　左一裏千家　玄関へのアフローチ　　右一裏千家の玄関

Naka-kuguri (window-gate), Omote Senke school of tea, Kyoto

Detail of main entrance, Ura Senke school of tea, Kyoto　　左—表千家　露路の中潜　　右—裏千家　玄関の上り段

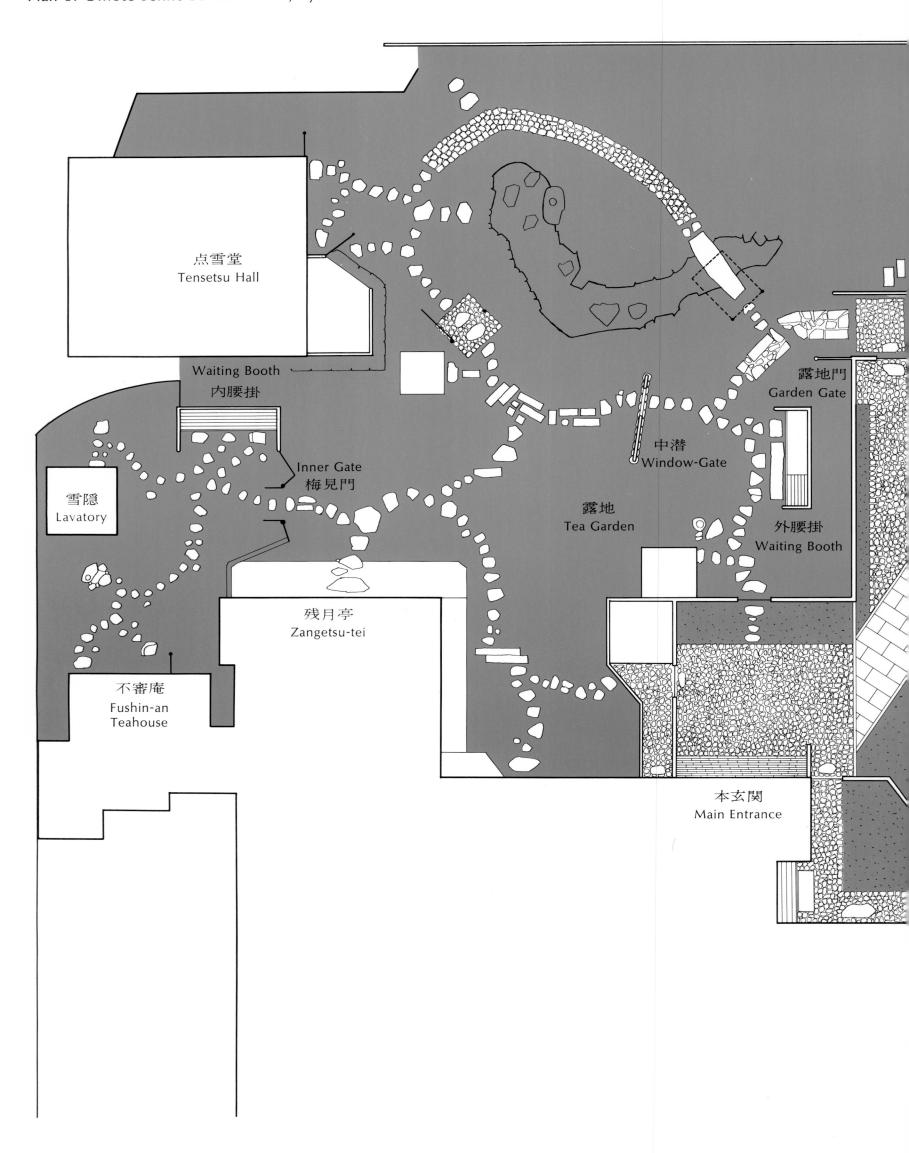

点雪堂
Tensetsu Hall

Waiting Booth
内腰掛

Inner Gate
梅見門

雪隠
Lavatory

残月亭
Zangetsu-tei

不審庵
Fushin-an
Teahouse

露地門
Garden Gate

中潜
Window-Gate

露地
Tea Garden

外腰掛
Waiting Booth

本玄関
Main Entrance

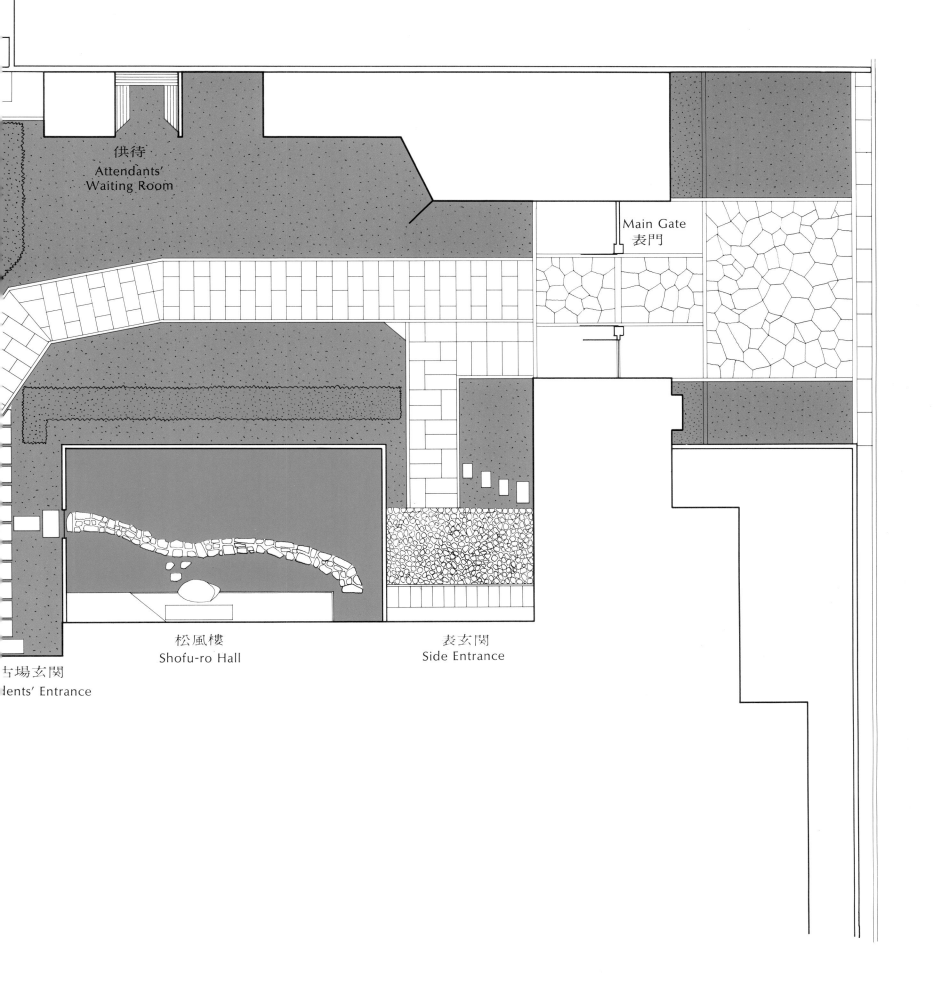

See photographs on pages 54-55, 116, 120-21, 124, 140, 152-53, 182-83. Omote Senke is both a school of the tea ceremony and the residence of the current master of the school.

供待
Attendants'
Waiting Room

Main Gate
表門

松風樓
Shofu-ro Hall

表玄関
Side Entrance

古場玄関
dents' Entrance

Detail of tiled roof

2. Conciseness of Composition

The thatched roof, the shingled roof, the tile roof, the clay wall, broad eaves, unpainted wood as a basic material, and undecorated construction—all these characteristic elements of the sukiya style give evidence of how much it resembles the minka. Since the teahouse originated in the minka, it can be said that construction in the sukiya style is essentially designed to reflect the minka style, but of course it is not a direct copy of that style. While the minka embodied a number of elements symbolic of the social level of its inhabitants, there was no such symbolism in sukiya construction. Instead, the sukiya building symbolized the aesthetic consciousness of the tea masters and expressed their ideals of wabi and sabi—that is, the "rustic simplicity" and "flavor of age" that we have previously noted. It is undoubtedly because of this—its rejection of symbols of social rank—that the sukiya style was able to survive despite changing social conditions.

As an example of status symbols in minka construction we may take the ridge covers used on the thatched roof. Originally such covers were placed at the points where the bundles of thatch that formed the ridge were tied with twine. There was a purely functional reason for this, since the twine could absorb rain water and allow it to leak into the house if no covers were provided. During the feudal period, however, the number of ridge covers on the roof came to be indicative of social status. The more there were, the higher the social rank of the inhabitants, and those who had the most were high-ranking officials such as village mayors. In the sukiya style, on the other hand, if a thatched roof was used, the style and number of ridge covers had no relationship to social status, and the covers were used purely for reasons of aesthetic design. Similarly, the gabled entrances found in many minka-style houses as status symbols had no place in the sukiya style, nor did such features of shoin and temple architecture as the heavy-tiled roof or the decorative covers at the ends of ridgepoles. All of these were alien to the concepts of wabi and sabi.

Just as the tea ceremony emphasizes natural beauty and natural creativeness (although, of course, it accents these in ways of its own), so the sukiya style emphasizes the natural beauty of the materials it employs. We must make the reservation, however, that "natural" here does not mean "primitive." For example, a newly cut log of cryptomeria, still covered with bark, will never be used in that state for a tokonoma post, not even when it is from one of the prized cryptomerias of Kyoto's Kitayama district. With great patience and much labor, its natural beauty will be brought out and accented. Similarly, although the ordinary clay wall of the minka has a certain charm, it will not do for the sukiya structure, since it is usually made of local clay in a purely functional fashion—that is, without concern for possible aesthetic values. The sukiya style recognizes the virtues of the clay wall, but it insists on a careful mixture of various clays to produce exactly the effect it desires. In this sense it makes of the minka clay wall an idealized reflection of nature. Again, in the case of the previously described shitaji-mado—the bamboo-lattice window—the sukiya style took its inspiration from the minka, refined what it found there, and then, interestingly enough, returned it to the minka in its new version.

In all of this—selection, rejection, borrowing, and refinement—the sukiya style was working toward a conciseness of statement and composition. The ideal of simplicity prevailed, even when the techniques themselves became more complicated than those used to produce the comparable features of the minka. Refinement, for the sukiya style, carried no connotations of elaboration.

The feature that decides the rhythm and order of the sukiya structure more than anything else is the post. We have observed that, except for the essential support at the four corners, the sukiya building is not subjected to the same strict arrangement of posts that we find in the minka. We have also noted that Isoya Yoshida, some forty years ago, set about to secure an even greater freedom for the sukiya structure in the placement of its posts. Until then, the placement had been more or less formalized by tradition and was a good deal more orderly than Yoshida liked. These posts, in comparison with those of the minka or the orthodox shoin style, were considerably more slim or at least managed to give an impression of slimness. Even the posts at Katsura, which are somewhat thicker than those of the usual sukiya structure, have a comparatively slim look. One reason for this is that they are longer than the ordinary sukiya post. Since the ceilings at Katsura are higher than usual, the posts had to be kept fairly large, but their length saves them from appearing heavy. Quite often the sukiya posts are socketed in natural stone, not only for the purpose of providing greater stability during earthquakes but also to add a sense of wabi and sabi.

The outer appearance of a building in sukiya style is quite simple and cheerful. There has obviously been an emancipation from the heaviness of construction in other traditional styles such as the minka and the shoin. While these two latter styles have a single roof system and a geometrically regular floor plan, the sukiya structure is free to move in directions of its own and to be quite irregular in its layout. Its roof system is similarly unorthodox and therefore, though more intricate, presents a light and airy appearance.

Although it lacks the monumentality and unity of the single roof system, it substitutes for these a sense of intimacy and a continuity of interesting changes among the various components of the structure. Minka and shoin roofs, like those of shrines and temples, impress the viewer with their strength and solidity, for they derive, after all, from the necessity of asserting status. The sukiya structure, on the other hand, having no such pretensions, need follow no predetermined style and may choose its roof system without restraint.

The simplicity and lightheartedness of the sukiya style are by no means the products of poverty or primitive artlessness, as has already become quite clear. The refinements that the style insists upon are neither easily created nor inexpensive. Its materials and their preparation are costly, and the services of highly trained craftsmen only add to the expense. Without these, however, there would be no sukiya style at all, and whatever structure might be created in its name would have neither stability nor refinement. In a word, the style itself is a product of the age of handicrafts in Japan, and the passing of that age is leaving it in a more and more precarious position. Nevertheless, its virtues are being emulated even today, and certainly not the least prized among them is its admirable concisensess of composition.

Ryokaku-tei teahouse, Ninna-ji, Kyoto　　仁和寺　遼廓亭の外観

◀ Kami no Chaya (Upper Teahouse) and view of garden, Shugaku-in villa, Kyoto

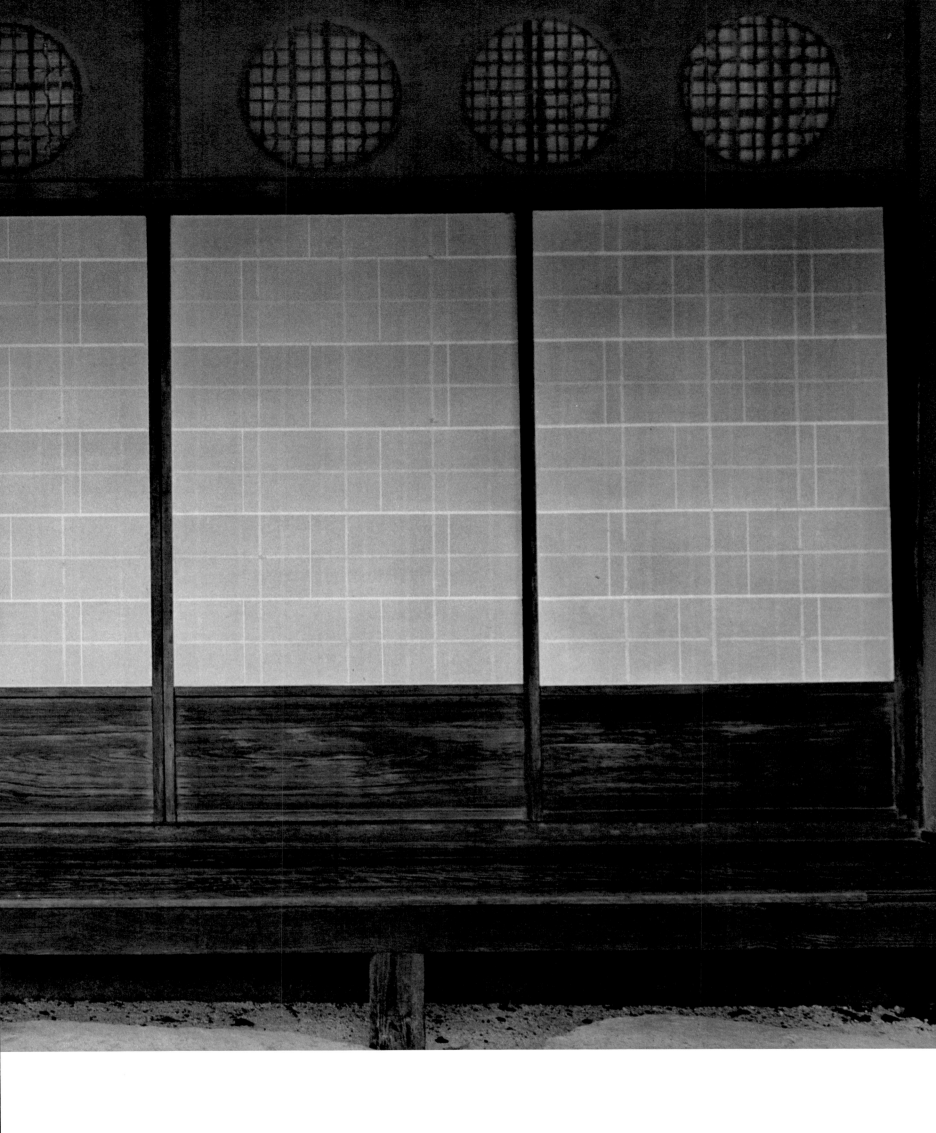

Detail of Shoi-ken teahouse, Katsura villa, Kyoto 桂離宮の笑意軒

桂離宮の笑意軒

◀ Shoi-ken teahouse, Katsura villa, Kyoto

Gable of Zangetsu-tei, Omote Senke school of tea, Kyoto

Detail of Shogetsu-tei teahouse, Sambo-in, Daigo-ji, Kyoto　左―表千家　残月亭の妻　　右―三宝院の松月亭

Shokin-tei teahouse, Katsura villa, Kyoto　　桂離宮　松琴亭の外観

Kikugetsu-tei, Ritsurin Park, Takamatsu　栗林公園の掬月亭

Kikugetsu-tei, Ritsurin Park, Takamatsu　栗林公園の掬月亭

Detail of veranda, Ryokaku-tei teahouse, Ninna-ji, Kyoto

Detail of abbot's residence, Sambo-in, Daigo-ji, Kyoto　　左—仁和寺　遼廓亭の縁　　右—三宝院書院の縁と束柱

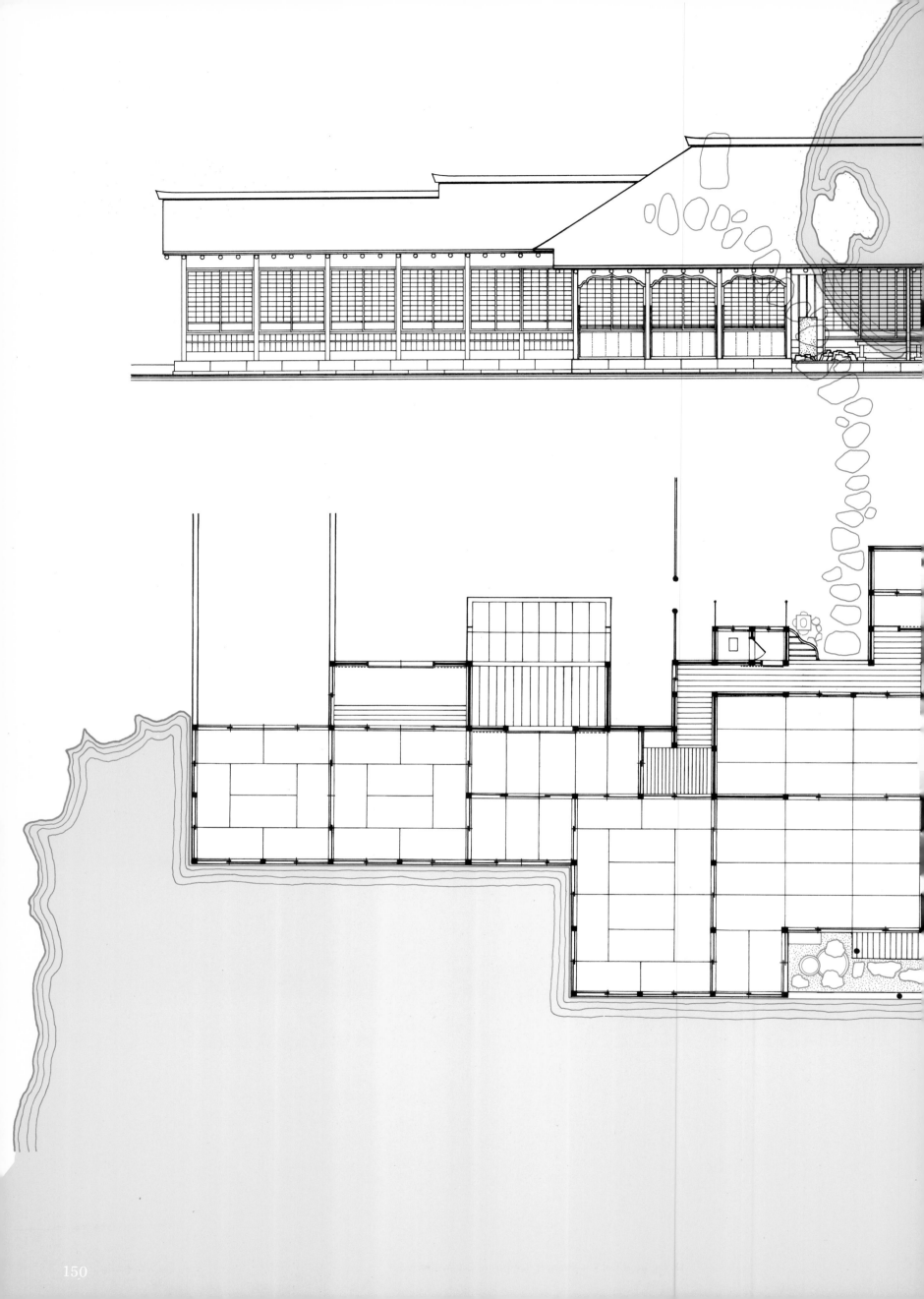

Plan of Yoko-kan, Fukui City 養浩館の西側立面図と平面図

The Yoko-kan, formerly part of the Matsudaira residence in Fukui City, was destroyed in the Pacific War. A brief description of it appears on page 73.

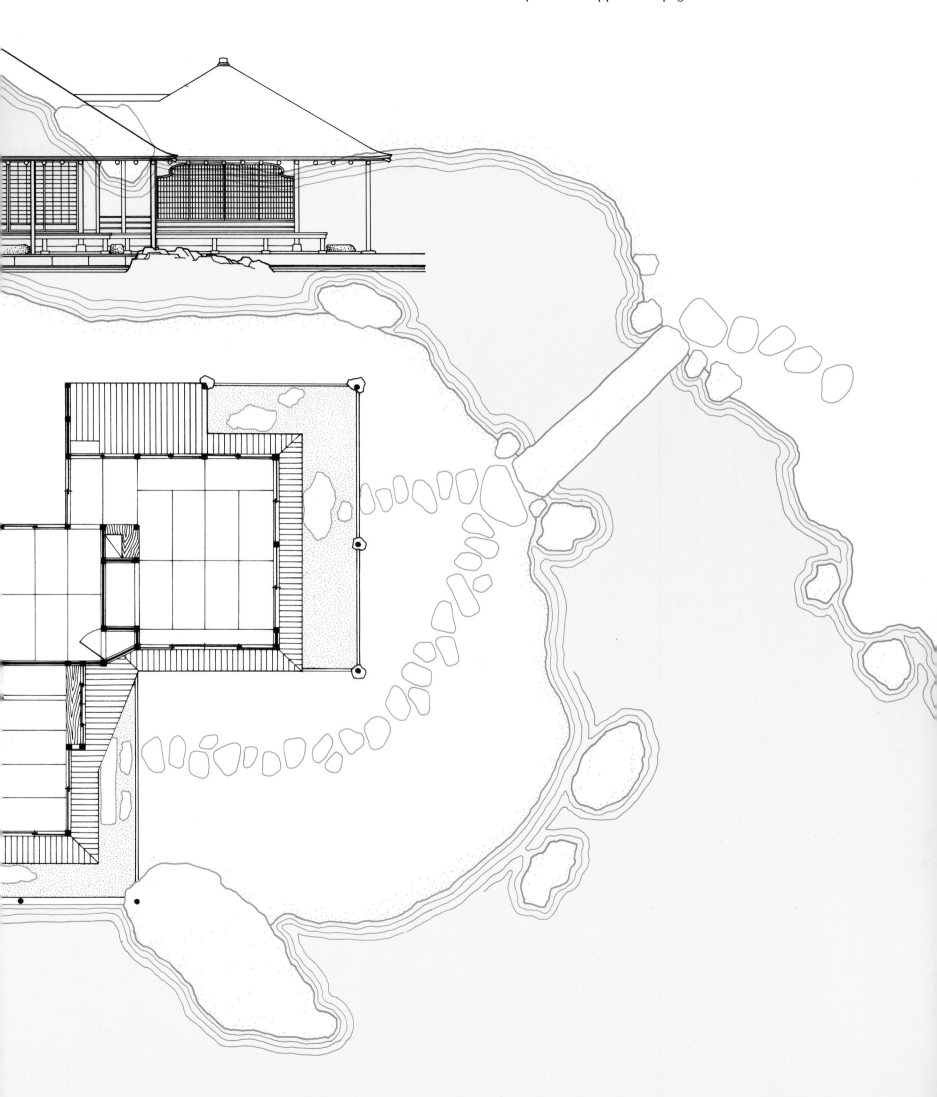

Detail of Fushin-an teahouse, Omote Senke school of tea, Kyoto 表千家　不審庵の躙口と下地窓

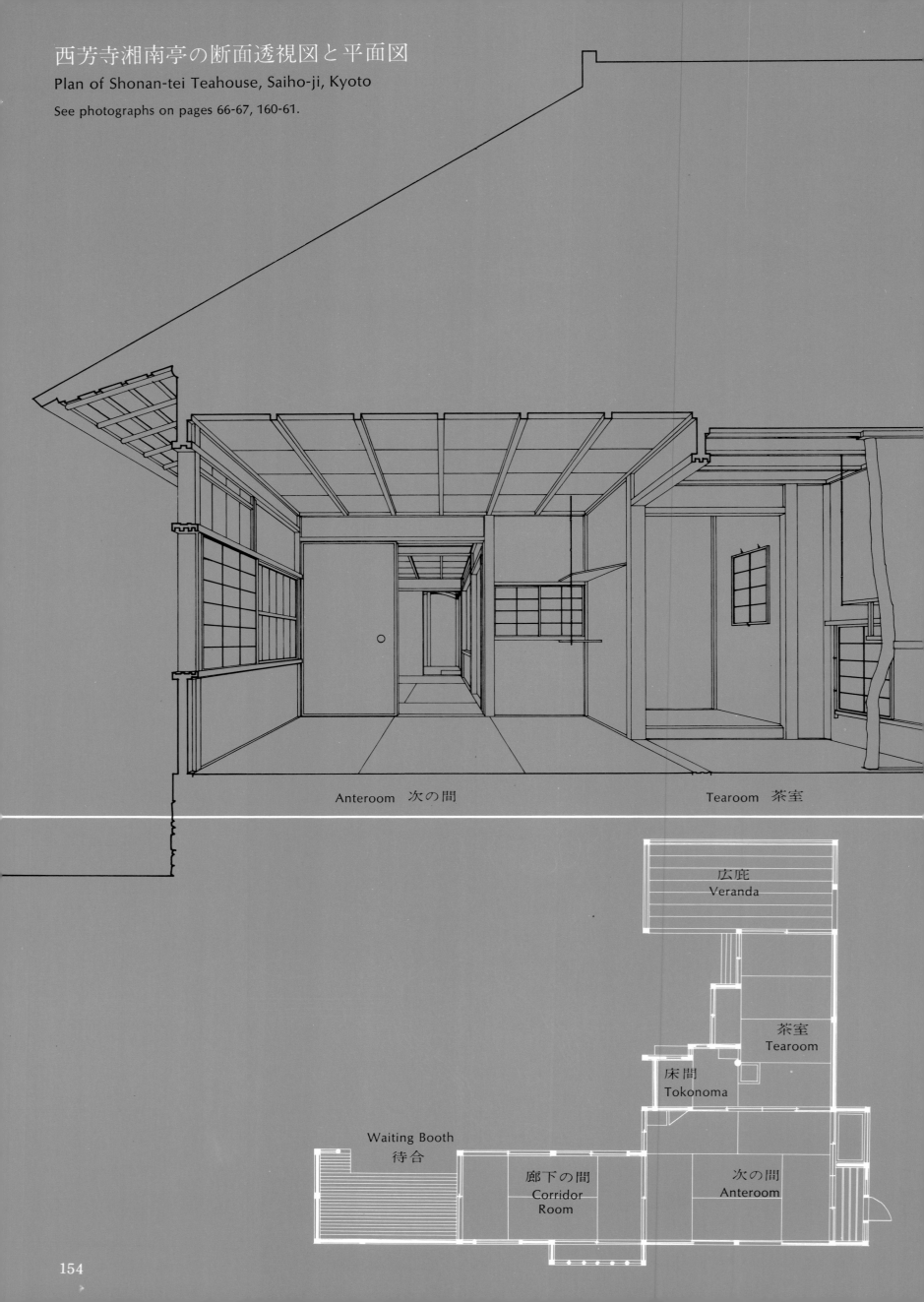

Anteroom　次の間

Tearoom　茶室

広庇
Veranda

茶室
Tearoom

床間
Tokonoma

Waiting Booth
待合

廊下の間
Corridor
Room

次の間
Anteroom

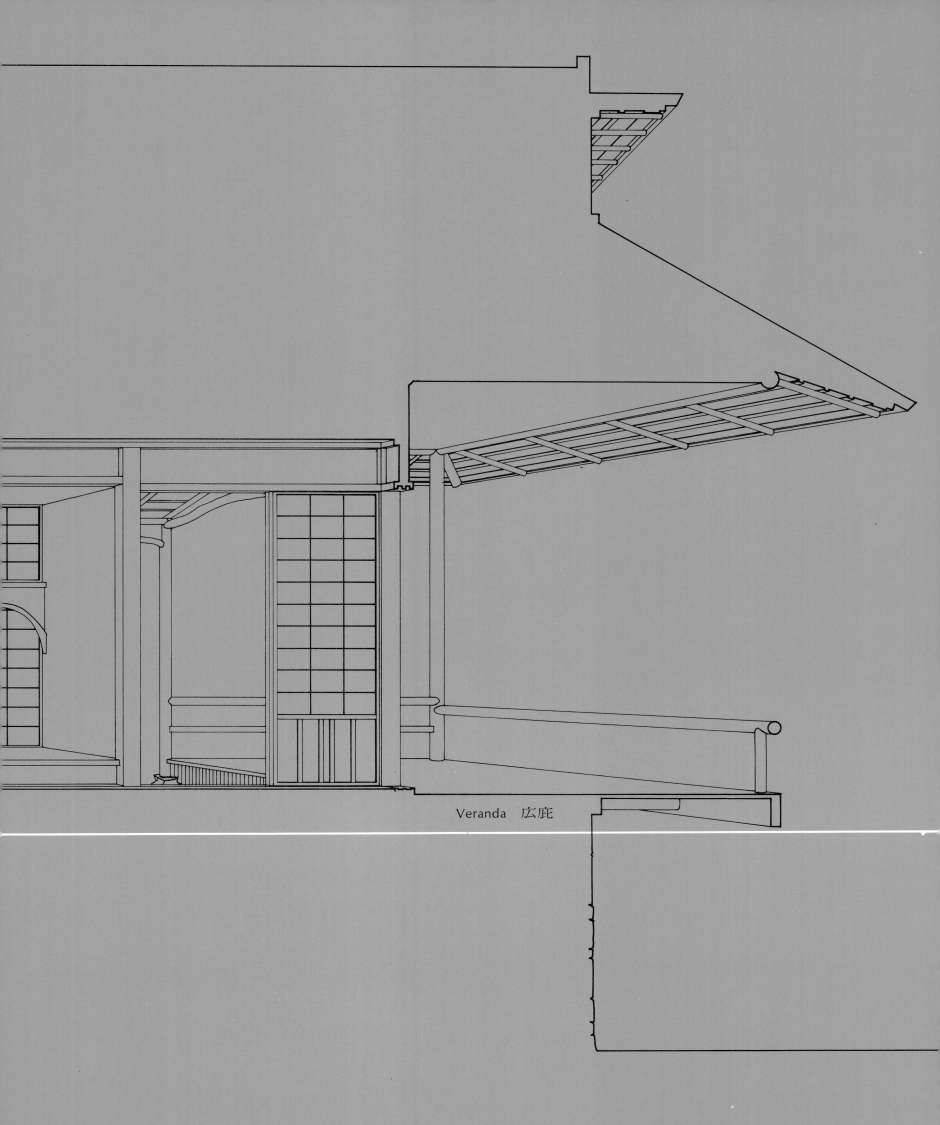

Veranda　広庇

3. Pivoting Space

A notable characteristic of the sukiya-style building is the unusual breadth of its eaves. Functionally, these broad eaves serve the purpose of protecting the building from destructive weathering and of helping to adjust the atmospheric conditions inside—for instance, by providing shade in summer. At the same time, in a perhaps more psychological than physical sense, the broad eaves and the area under them serve to unite interior and exterior space—in a word, to unite architecture with nature. This unification, needless to say, has great appeal for the Japanese and has long been a requirement of their traditional architecture. Since the area under the eaves plays a dual role, belonging to both interior and exterior, we may call it "pivoting space." The meaning of the term will become clear as we look more closely at this feature of sukiya architecture.

In the sukiya style this pivoting space has always been given great emphasis. Indeed it is here that the geometrical orderliness invented by man must have as harmonious a meeting as possible with the essential disorderliness of nature. To be sure, some type of order may be imposed upon the outdoor area (no Japanese garden, for example, is ever allowed to run riot), but essentially this area still represents nature. Traditional Western architecture makes a clean-cut separation of indoor and outdoor space, but traditional Japanese architecture declines to do this, for in Japanese thinking it represents a basic disharmony. Nature is not to be excluded but to be invited in. It will be worthwhile to examine this uniting of indoor and outdoor space more closely.

First of all, the eaves must be broad. The posts, beams, and rafters used there are often of cryptomeria. The depth of the eaves generally varies from about 3.5 feet to somewhat over 7 feet, but there are instances in which it reaches as much as 11 feet. Under the eaves there may be either a wooden veranda or an earthen floor or sometimes a combination of the two. Since there is no borderline between this area and the surrounding garden, we may regard the space as part of the garden itself. But in the sense that it affords protection from rain and strong sunlight it must be considered part of the building. Strictly speaking, however, it does not belong to either the interior or the exterior space. Its role is an intermediate one, and we must associate it with both its interior and its exterior advantages. In one way it serves as a protection against nature (rain and strong sunlight); in another, it makes nature more familiar. Actually there is nothing paradoxical in this role.

A large stone, usually accompanied by several others, is placed either in the earth-floored area or at the edge of the veranda to serve as a step for going outdoors (pages 32, 160–61). The sizes and shapes of these stones vary, and their arrangement is never symmetrical. This traditional pattern, of course, has many variations, both in the number and in the type of stones used. There may also be steppingstones leading into the garden in a diagonal or curved-line arrangement.

The earth floor under the eaves is not simply an area of unplanted ground. It is usually composed of a special Kyoto clay mixed with lime. In former times, oil and salt were added to the mixture to make it more compact. At the outer edge of this area a gutter is often constructed to catch the rain which drips from the eaves (pages 19, 93). It may be of rather formal design, perhaps with stone edges, or it may be merely a border of pebbles filling a shallow trench. Various types of stones are used for the gutter, and occasionally sections of roof tile or even a bed of charcoal may be substituted. The purpose here, of course, is to keep the ground from being muddy underfoot, especially in seasons of heavy rainfall.

The space under the eaves may also be used for a veranda (pages 30–31, 144–45), and occasionally, as in the instance of the moon-viewing veranda at Katsura (pages 166–67), the structure may be extended into the area outside the line of the eaves. The veranda floor may be of bamboo or wood, but in either case it is never painted. Natural aging and frequent use give the flooring material an added beauty, bringing out the grain in wood and adding luster to both wood and bamboo. Like the sukiya building itself, the floor is not at its best when it is new. In fact, for the Japanese, a newly finished sukiya building is only at the beginning of the true beauty that it will later acquire, as time, nature, and human use play their roles, and in this concept we see reflected again the ideals of the earliest sukiya designers: a high regard for aesthetic values created through the long processes of time. When, for example, we consider the grain in the wood of the veranda at Katsura as an artistic pattern created by time and nature and not only as an element of refined construction, its beauty comes to have greater value.

Nor should we ignore purely physical factors, for the materials of construction have much to do with our sense of comfort and pleasure. It is interesting to note for instance, that Japanese cypress has long been favored as a flooring material for verandas. For some reason, when one sits on a cypress-floored veranda, he tends to have a feeling of mental and physical tranquility. Much of this, to be sure, is a psychological reaction occasioned by the long familiarity of the Japanese with an architectural tradition. Cypress is right for a veranda floor, one thinks, and one is more comfortable with cypress than with anything else. Oddly enough, recent scientific research has added another explanation: in comparison with other materials, Japanese cypress is considerably less capable of reflecting ultraviolet rays. Perhaps, then, the preference for cypress has more than just a psychological foundation.

In earlier times, the veranda was never enclosed and was thus not treated as part of the interior space. Today, however, glass sliding doors are usually installed at the outer edge, and sometimes the floor is covered with tatami to create what the Japanese call an *en-zashiki* or veranda room. Thus the veranda actually becomes an integral part of the room, particularly in winter, when the glass doors are closed. This change in its role came about because of the increasing availability and cheapness of glass as time went on.

The glass doors of the veranda, the sliding wooden shutters outside them that enclose the house at night, and the translucent shoji that substitute for walls are all mobile partitions which serve to separate interior and exterior as occasion demands. The wooden shutters, in addition to deterring housebreakers, protect the interior from violent wind and heavy rain, particularly in the summer and autumn typhoon season. At the same time they help to maintain the inside temperature in winter and to reduce indoor humidity. The shoji, on the contrary, absorb outdoor temperature and humidity and thus play no protective role unless it be that of preventing drafts. The glass doors, while they tend to shut off outdoor humidity and cold, absorb light and heat. But the combination of these three forms of the mobile partition permits a rather remarkable control of interior atmospheric conditions. Again, not only do they serve as partitions, for they are entrances and exits as well, and they may readily be moved out of the way. The shutters slide into a special compartment at one end of the veranda. The shoji and the glass doors may be slid over one another or lifted out and stored away. In a Western-style building, a window, no matter how large, is not generally considered to be an entrance or an exit, but the mobile partitions of the traditional Japanese house serve as both windows and doors.

It is their mobility, of course, which enables these sliding partitions to play their role in the merging of indoor and outdoor space. Unlike solid walls, or even walls supplied with an abundance of doors and windows, they form no permanent boundary between outdoors and indoors, either physical or psychological. When they are closed, it is only for the sake of convenience, and they may be readily opened to enlarge the living space and permit free and intimate contact with nature. They are thus an important part of the concept of pivoting space.

We have already noted that the shoji have an essential role in creating the atmosphere of a room, but it will not be amiss here to look once again at the versatility with which they perform this function. When they are closed on a cool day, they serve as a kind of screen on which the silhouettes of trees and other outdoor objects may appear. When the two central panels of the customary set of four shoji are opened, the garden is viewed in the manner of a framed picture. In the heat of summer all four panels may be lifted out and a bamboo blind hung in their place, so that the room seems to become a part of the outdoor space, while the breeze is allowed to sweep freely into the house. In winter, if the house is furnished with snow-viewing shoji, the lower panels of glass may be exposed by raising the paper panels that cover them, and the outdoor scene can be viewed without discomfort from the cold. The invention of the snow-viewing shoji, in fact, enlarged the space-presentation repertoire of the sukiya style without in the least violating its concepts of beauty.

This, in turn, suggests that the true virtue of the sukiya style lies not in its concern with the refinement of architectural detail but in its spatial concepts, and in this respect, of course, it is eminently modern in its outlook and its applicability. Certainly its concept of pivoting space, so widely admired by architects today, is a major element of its modernity.

Detail of Shonan-tei teahouse, Saiho-ji, Kyoto ▶

西芳寺　湘南亭の縁

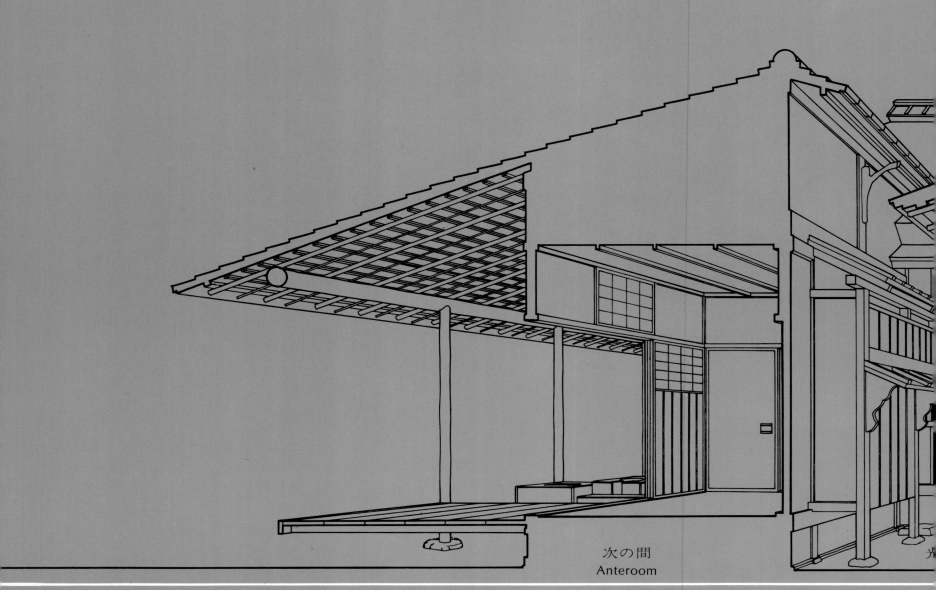

次の間
Anteroom

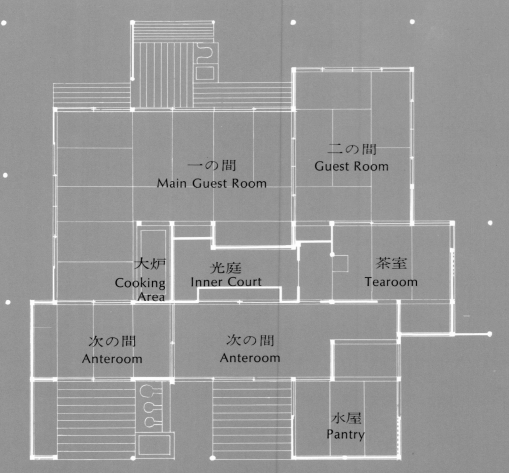

一の間
Main Guest Room

二の間
Guest Room

大炉
Cooking
Area

光庭
Inner Court

茶室
Tearoom

次の間
Anteroom

次の間
Anteroom

水屋
Pantry

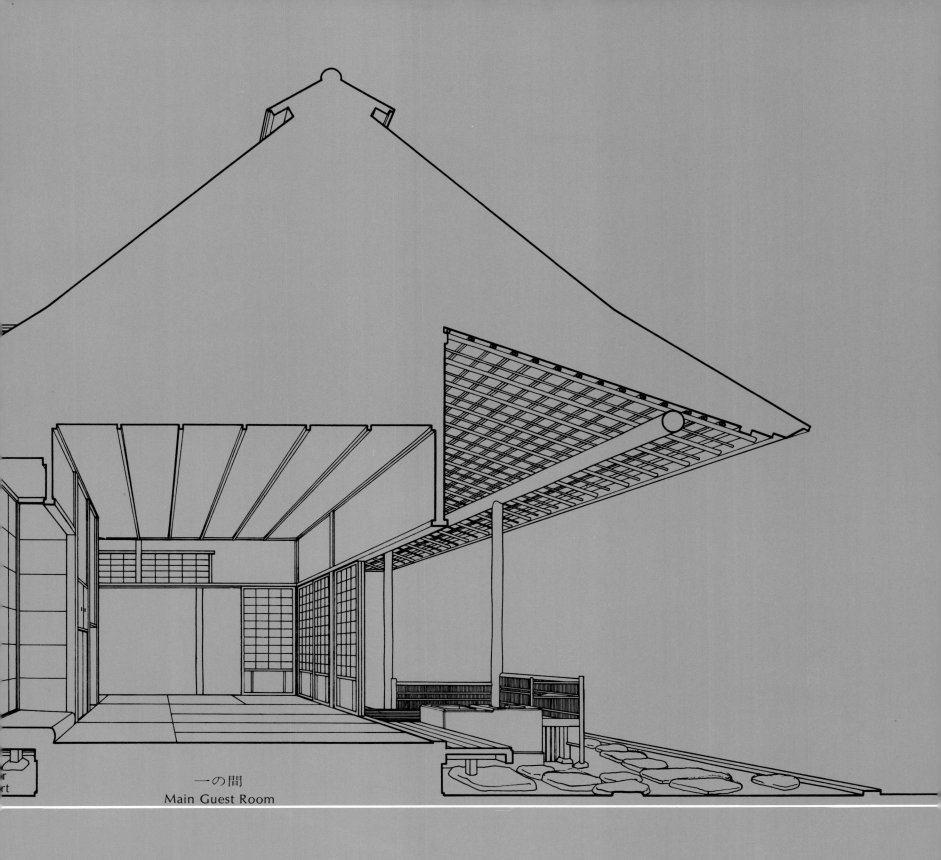

一の間
Main Guest Room

Veranda, Shokin-tei
teahouse, Katsura villa,
Kyoto

桂離宮　松琴亭の土庇

Moon-viewing veranda, Katsura villa, Kyoto

桂離宮　古書院の月見台

Detail of Koho-an, Daitoku-ji, Kyoto　孤篷庵　忘筌の間の縁

◀ Ryu-tei pavilion, Koraku-en, Okayama City

Detail of veranda, Black Shoin, Nishi Hongan-ji, Kyoto

Detail of Teigyoku-ken teahouse, Shinju-an, Daitoku-ji, Kyoto 　左—西本願寺　黒書院の縁と竹垣　　右—真珠庵　庭玉軒の蹲踞と下地窓

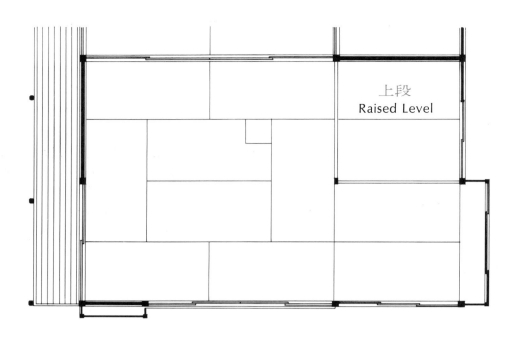

残月亭の現状平面図
Floor Plan of Present Zangetsu-tei

上段
Raised Level

入側
Tatami Veranda

N

利休聚楽屋敷の九間の図
Floor Plan of Rikyu's Colored
Shoin at Juraku-dai

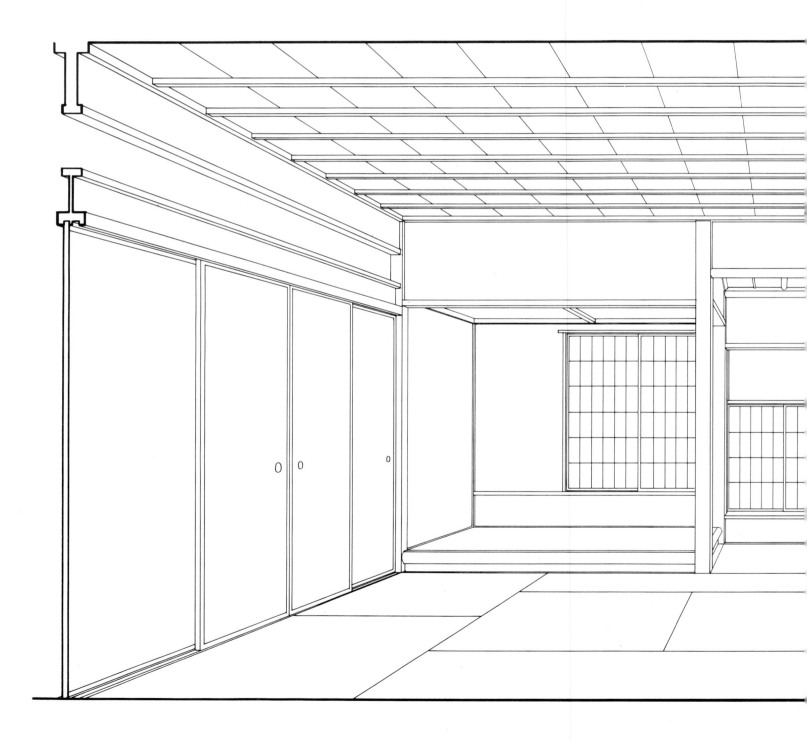

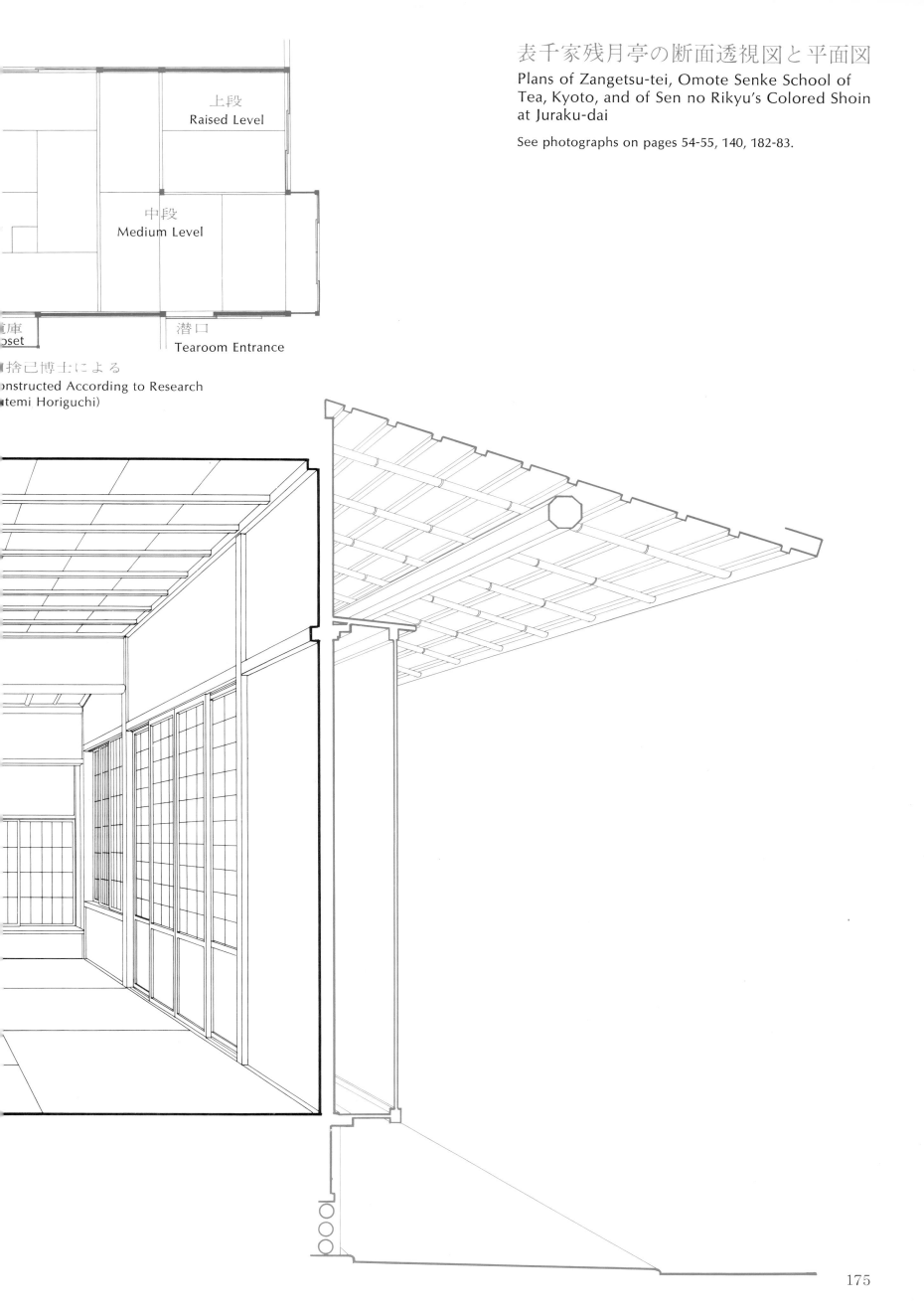

上段
Raised Level

中段
Medium Level

潜口
Tearoom Entrance

庫
oset

捨己博士による

onstructed According to Research
temi Horiguchi)

表千家残月亭の断面透視図と平面図

Plans of Zangetsu-tei, Omote Senke School of
Tea, Kyoto, and of Sen no Rikyu's Colored Shoin
at Juraku-dai

See photographs on pages 54-55, 140, 182-83.

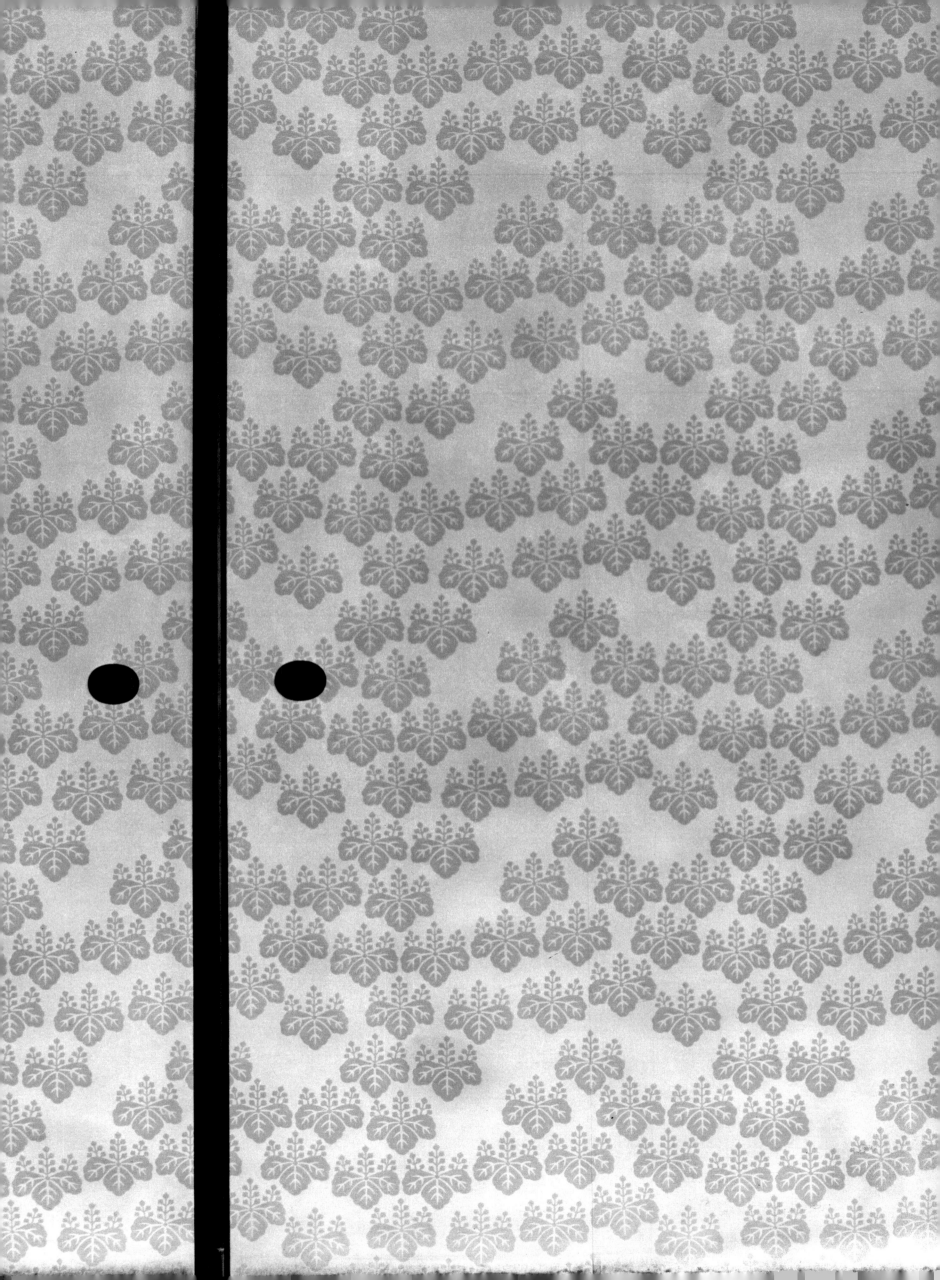

4. The Flexible Interior

Like the shoji and the other movable partitions that open to the exterior, the tatami and the fusuma have an important function in determining the spatial arrangements in Japanese architecture, as much in the sukiya style as in any other traditional style. They are essential elements of what we may call the flexible interior—that is, the interior which adapts itself to any number of purposes and spatial patterns.

The role of the tatami in traditional Japanese architecture is hardly less versatile than that of the shoji. At first glance this reed-covered mat of rice straw may appear to be no more than a rather appealing type of floor covering, but this is only one of its functions. It also serves as an insulation against cold air beneath the house, which of course has no basement. Again, in the relatively furnitureless Japanese house, it serves as a place to sit, a place to sleep, and even a place to dance in Japanese style. The tatami-floored room may be a living room, a dining room, a guest room, a bedroom, or a conference hall. We have already observed the essential role of the tatami as a basic unit for determining the spatial order within a building—not only the size of rooms but also the proportions of their various elements: the height of the lintels, for example, and the height of the ceiling. The area of the tokonoma almost always equals that of one tatami, and the measurements of the shelves adjoining the tokonoma, of closets, of corridors, and even of shoji and fusuma are all decided in terms of the tatami unit.

Usually the size of the tatami is the same for all rooms, and, as we have noted earlier, houses in western Japan have traditionally used the tatami system for their floor plans. In general, this means that the floor area is decided in multiples of the standard-size tatami. One of the characteristics of the sukiya style, however, is that its free system of basic planning often produces spaces that are not of standard tatami size. Such irregularities, of course, are not accidental and therefore pose no problems. The spaces are skillfully used as sections of wooden or earthen floor, for tokonoma of unorthodox size, or for closets. It goes without saying that the sukiya-style room thereby gains in individuality and charm. Even in the relatively few sukiya structures that employ the post system of basic planning, the size of the tatami does not vary, and the measurements of the details (tokonoma, shelves, and the like) are still decided in terms of the tatami grid.

The Western reader may be surprised to learn that there is also a quite rigid etiquette of the tatami-floored room. For example, it is considered ill-bred to step on the edges of the tatami or to seat oneself without regard to one's position in relation to the edges. To be precise, in the formal kneeling position one's knees should be approximately sixteen rows of stitches from the edge. Similar rules apply to the placement of objects on the tatami on such occasions as the tea ceremony. Some are placed inside the edge *(heri-uchi)* and some outside *(heri-soto)* in relation to one's seated position. There is no need to expand upon this subject here, since it is, after all, rather esoteric, and since any number of modern Japanese violate the etiquette, but it is interesting nevertheless that the tatami itself should have inspired such a detailed code of manners.

It would be deceptive to say that the sukiya style of architecture employs only movable partitions, for the clay wall is also a part of it. The tokonoma is always backed by a wall, and other sections of the room may also be walled. Essentially, though, the sukiya room is enclosed by such mobile partitions as shoji and fusuma, the latter serving as interior room dividers. The virtue of the fusuma, like that of the shoji, is that they can be removed to create a larger space or, in summer, to allow complete ventilation of the house. On special occasions—perhaps a large family gathering or a banquet at an inn—several rooms can be converted into a single hall-like space. Again, depending upon the season or the type of gathering, the fusuma can be replaced with others of appropriate color or design. Although fusuma in other styles of Japanese architecture may be decorated with representational paintings, as were those in the residences of the feudal-period aristocracy, in the sukiya style they are quite plain or, at most, display modest patterns. The preferred colors are light green, lavender, light blue, and a kind of terra cotta. In a word, vivid colors are rejected in favor of neutral ones that may not be noticed at all. While the ornately painted fusuma of the shoin style sought to emphasize the social standing of feudal aristocrats and to impress the viewer as symbols of affluence and power, the unobtrusive fusuma of the sukiya style were designed as a background for the people who used the room and as a means of enhancing their pleasure in comfortable surroundings. Fusuma of striking color and lavish design call attention to themselves and away from those who use the room, and this, of course, is quite opposite to the intention of the the sukiya style. As several Edo-period books say of the tea garden, no feature should be too attractive or too noticeable, and sukiya-style architecture has taken this injunction to heart.

In the same manner the shoji and the clay wall are not allowed to be obtrusive. Although there are a number of variations of the basic shoji grid—for example, the grid which employs more vertical strips than horizontal ones and thus produces tall, narrow rectangles and a more crowded design—the sukiya style prefers a simpler grid with fewer horizontal and vertical strips and larger white spaces. Since the clay wall is unsuitable for painting in any case, it remains quite plain and displays only the natural beauty of the materials from which it is made. These materials, as we have seen, are carefully selected and combined. To the modern eye such walls have a chic and up-to-date appearance, even though we may remember that the sukiya style borrowed the idea from the teahouse some four centuries ago.

The formal guest room of the typical sukiya structure has a tokonoma, *chigai-dana* (shelves placed at two levels on a diagonal line) next to the tokonoma, and a *tsuke-shoin*—that is, a window with a broad sill some two feet above the floor. Although the chigai-dana and the tsuke-shoin are sometimes omitted, the tokonoma is always there, for it is the invariable symbol of the guest room. Quite often superb wood or bamboo is selected for its main post, but the post is never decorated with lacquer or other materials as in the shoin style. The most typical tokonoma post in the sukiya style is of polished wood which retains its natural look but at the same time gives a sense of refinement and lightness. Although in the earliest days of its history the tokonoma appears to have been a place for the honored guest to sit, it now serves for the display of a painting, an art object, or a flower arrangement. The sukiya-style room furnishes no other place for such display, and since tatami, walls, fusuma, and ceiling are undecorated, the tokonoma naturally serves as a focus for attention. It is hardly necessary to point out that excessive display of paintings on walls and of art objects in numerous places destroys the unity of the interior design, whether it be in a Western-style room or (and this is much less imaginable) one in Japanese style. In the sukiya style the tokonoma plays the important role of giving unity to the interior design, since it is the only place allowed for decoration of this type.

Most of this we have observed before, but it is not irrelevant here to stress once again the role of the tokonoma in relation to the other elements of interior design, for it too, though immobile, is capable of changing the scene. In the painting, the art object, or the flower arrangement placed there, the guest sees reflected not only the taste of his host and a subtle compliment to his own taste but also the season of the year and the significance of the occasion. Naturally, then, the host must give considerable thought to the tokonoma decorations, for the discerning guest will be sure to judge them in the light of their appropriateness. At the same time these decorations play a major part in creating the atmosphere of the room and the occasion and in making the guest feel welcome and at ease. It is difficult to overemphasize the role of the tokonoma in this respect. Although it is a fixed feature of the room, it is nevertheless a part of the flexible interior, since, through its decorations, it is hardly less capable of giving the room a new appearance than the movable fusuma and shoji.

Interior of Kyusui-ken pavilion, Shugaku-in villa, Kyoto ▶

179

修学院離宮　窮邃軒の内部

Interior of Zangetsu-tei, Omote Senke school of tea, Kyoto　残 月 亭

Interior of guest room, Shokin-tei teahouse, Katsura villa, Kyoto　桂離宮　松琴亭の内部

Circular window, Shogetsu-tei teahouse, Sambo-in, Daigo-ji, Kyoto　　三宝院　松月亭の丸窓

Yukimi (snow-viewing) shoji and bamboo-floored veranda, Hassho-kan restaurant, Nagoya　　八勝館　中店の縁と雪見障子

Tokonoma, Kan'in tearoom, Juko-in, Kyoto

Detail of Hasso no Seki, Nanzen-ji, Kyoto　　左—聚光院　閑隠席の床間　　右—金地院　八窓の席の内部

Tokonoma and adjoining shelves and closet, Ryokaku-tei teahouse, Ninna-ji, Kyoto　　仁和寺　遼廓亭の床間

Detail of Mushiki-ken tearoom, Ura Senke school of tea, Kyoto

Shoji in shoin, Katsura villa, Kyoto　左—裏千家　無色軒の内部　右—桂離宮　書院の障子

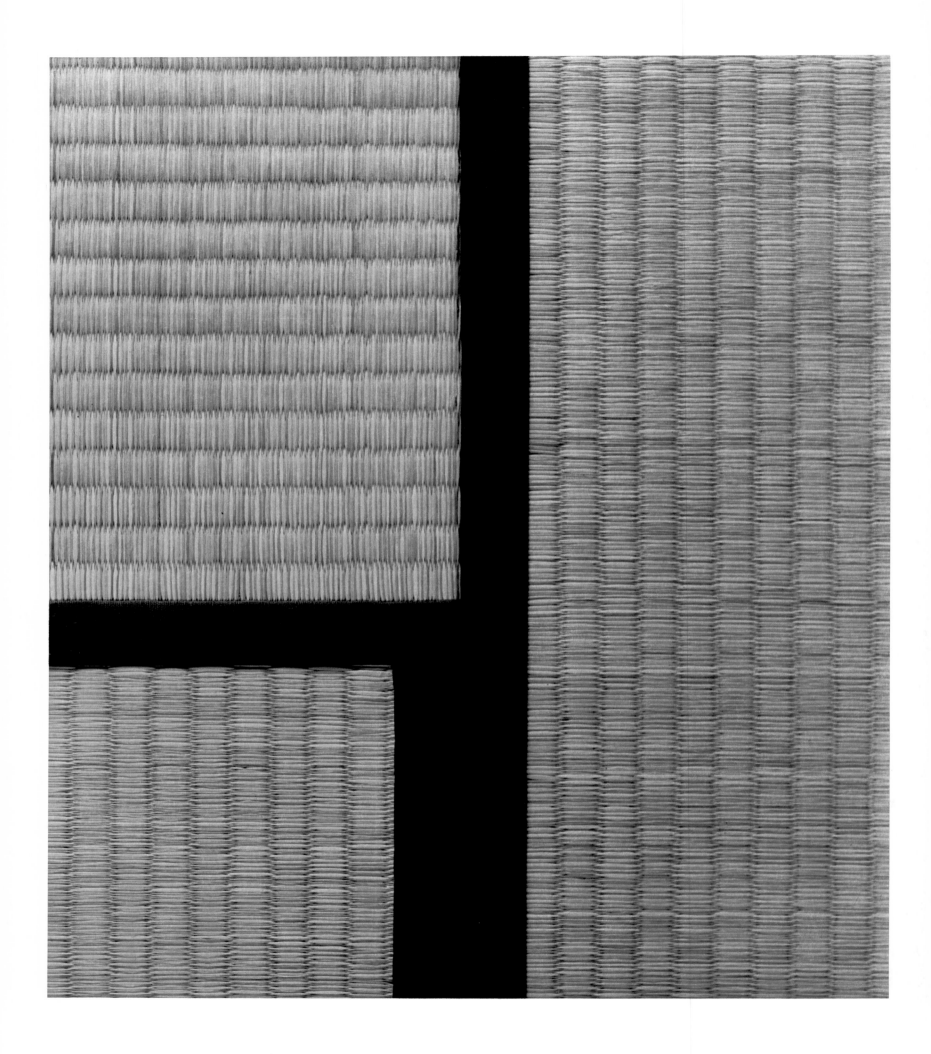

Detail of tatami floor

Tearoom charcoal pit　　左―畳　右―炉

Reed shoji and reed blinds

Detail of yukimi (snow-viewing) shoji and inner garden, Kitcho Restaurant, Osaka　　左—簾　　右—吉兆の雪見障子と坪庭

Ceiling, Geppa-ro pavilion, Katsura villa, Kyoto

Detail of ceiling, Hasso no Seki, Nanzen-ji, Kyoto

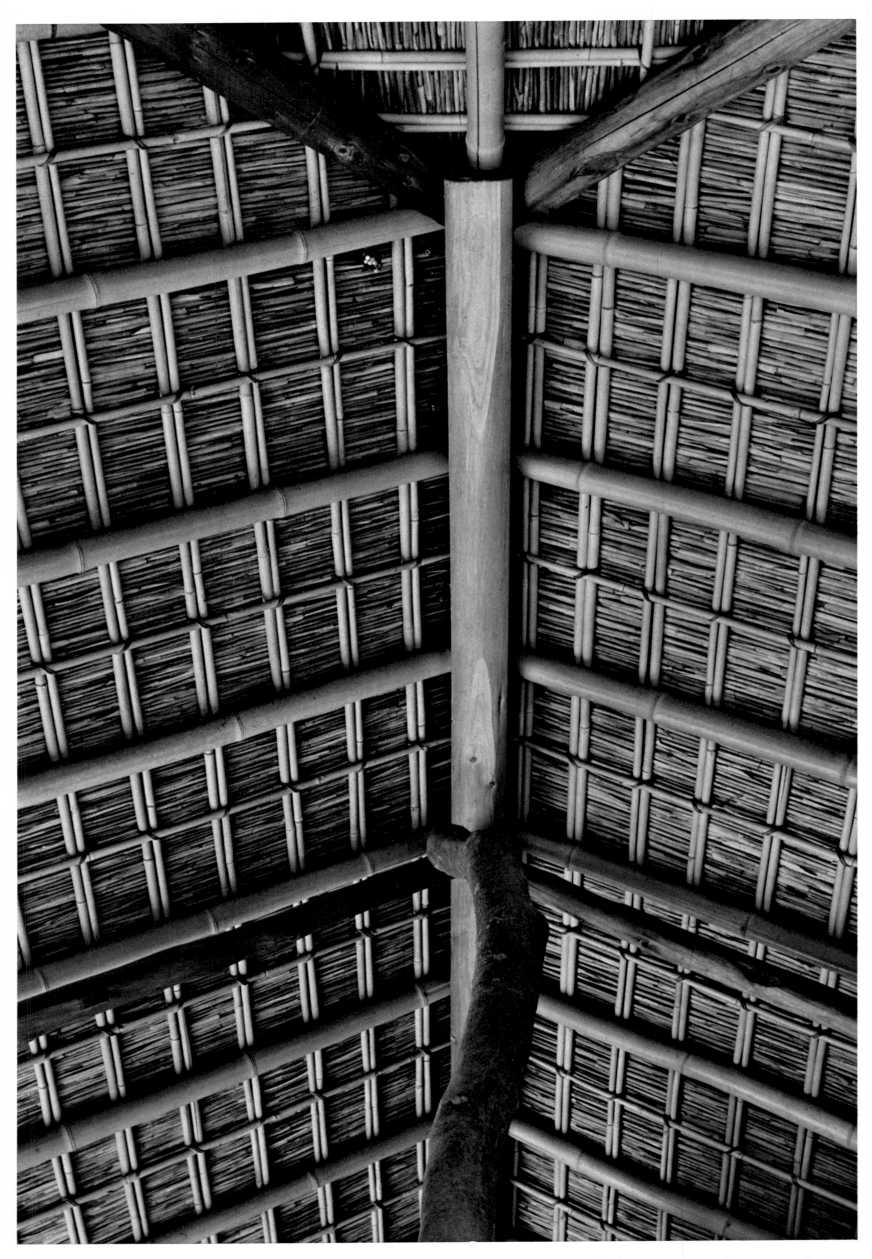

Detail of ceiling, Geppa-ro pavilion, Katsura villa, Kyoto

Reference Matter

Acknowledgments

It is time, now, to express my sincere gratitude to the numerous persons and organizations whose generous help made this book possible. The order in which they are mentioned has no special significance, for the effort was a truly cooperative one, and every contribution had its own indispensable part to play in the final realization of the project.

The most difficult task of all was the preparation of the architectural drawings that accompany the photographs. Drawings of this general type are by no means uncommon, for they appear quite frequently in any number of publications, but they are usually full of errors, and it would have been impossible to use any of them. It was necessary to remeasure all the buildings and to make new drawings. In the process it was decided to use several styles of presentation in order to make it easier for the reader to understand and appreciate the structures shown. Even the briefest glance at these drawings will make it clear that no ordinary talent could have produced them. I was fortunate indeed to have the help of three experts: Mr. Mitsuru Suzuki, Mr. Shunsuke Itoh, and Mr. Hironari Kanno. None of these three young men could be described as a mere draftsman. Mr. Suzuki is an architectural historian, and Mr. Itoh and Mr. Kanno are both well versed in traditional and modern architecture. Their assistance, it goes without saying, was invaluable.

I have known Mr. Yukio Futagawa for a long time —since the days, in fact, when he was an unknown photographer. We understand each other without the need of words, and we employed this same telepathic communication in the preparation of our two earlier works, *The Roots of Japanese Architecture* and *The Essential Japanese House*. It was also my good fortune to have the services of Mr. Ikko Tanaka, who has so successfully translated the image of the sukiya style in the layout and design of the book and has, in fact, perfectly realized my original concept.

I wish to express my heartfelt thanks to the organizations which made it possible to take the photographs and prepare the architectural drawings needed for the book: the Kyoto Office of the Imperial Household; the Omote and the Ura Senke schools of the tea ceremony; the maintenance offices of the Okayama Koraku-en, Ritsurin Park, and the Sankei-en garden; the temples Ninna-ji, Nishi Hongan-ji, and Saiho-ji; the abbots' residences of Gyokurin-in, Juko-in, Koho-an, Konchi-in, Sambo-in, and Shinju-an; the restaurants Hassho-kan, Ichiriki-tei, Kitcho, and Minoko; and the Miyako Hotel. Again, I am deeply indebted to Mr. Kinjiro Kitamura for the permission to photograph his residence in detail.

My special gratitude goes to Mr. Shiro Usui, editor, and to Mr. Koshiro Ozasa, assistant editor, of Tanko Shinsha, the original Japanese publishers of the book. I am also grateful to the editorial staff of John Weatherhill, Inc., for the understanding way they have translated my text and, in consultation with me, adapted it for Western readers—particularly to Miss Miriam F. Yamaguchi, who began the difficult translation, and to Mr. Ralph Friedrich, who is responsible for the final English version.

TEIJI ITOH

Locations of Outstanding Sukiya-Style Buildings

Arizawa Sanso villa: Sugata-cho, Matsue, Shimane Prefecture

* Black Shoin (Kuro Shoin): Nishi Hongan-ji, Hanaya-cho-sagaru, Horikawa, Shimokyo-ku, Kyoto

Choryu-tei pavilion: Enuma Shrine, Daishoji-cho, Kaga, Ishikawa Prefecture

Fukiage-chaya: Rikugi-en villa, Fujimae-cho, Bunkyo-ku, Tokyo

* Fushin-an teahouse: Omote Senke school of tea, Teranouchi, Ogawa-dori, Kamikyo-ku, Kyoto

* Geppa-ro pavilion: Katsura villa, Katsura Misono-cho, Ukyo-ku, Kyoto

* Hassho-kan restaurant: Yagoto, Mizuho-ku, Nagoya

* Hasso no Seki: abbot's residence, Konchi-in, Nanzen-ji, Nanzenji Fukuchi-machi, Sakyo-ku, Kyoto

Hekiun-so: Shimogawara-machi, Nanzenji, Sakyo-ku, Kyoto

Hyo-tei pavilion: 35 Kusakawa-cho, Nanzenji, Sakyo-ku, Kyoto

* Ichiriki-tei restaurant: Gion, Higashiyama-ku, Kyoto

* Kami no Chaya: Shugaku-in villa, Shugakuin, Sakyo-ku, Kyoto

Kangetsu-an: Izu, Atami, Shizuoka Prefecture

* Kan'in tearoom: abbot's residence, Juko-in, Daitoku-ji, Daitokuji-cho, Murasakino, Kita-ku, Kyoto

Kantoku-tei pavilion: Koraku-en, Koishikawa, Bunkyo-ku, Kyoto

* Kasui-en: Miyako Hotel, Sanjo Keage, Higashiyama-ku, Kyoto

* Katsura villa: Katsura Misono-cho, Ukyo-ku, Kyoto

* Kikugetsu-tei and Shoen-kan: Ritsurin Park, Ritsurin-cho, Takamatsu, Kagawa Prefecture

Kinka-ryo: Omiya Shichijo, Shimokyo-ku, Kyoto

* Kitamura residence: Imadegawa Kajii-cho, Kawara-machi, Kamikyo-ku, Kyoto

Kitcho Restaurant (Kyoto): Tenryuji, Saga, Ukyo-ku, Kyoto

* Kitcho Restaurant (Osaka): Korai-bashi, 2-chome, Higashi-ku, Osaka

Kobun-tei pavilion: Kairaku-en, Tokiwa-cho, Mito, Ibaraki Prefecture

* Koho-an: abbot's residence, Daitoku-ji, Daitokuji-cho, Murasakino, Kita-ku, Kyoto

Kokin-denju shoin house: Joju-en, Suizenji, Izumi-cho, Kumamoto City, Kumamoto Prefecture

* Konnichi-an tearoom: Ura Senke school of tea, Teranouchi, Ogawa-dori, Kamikyo-ku, Kyoto

* Kyusui-ken pavilion: Shugaku-in villa, Shugakuin, Sakyo-ku, Kyoto

* Minoko Restaurant: Gion Kiyoi-cho, Shimogawara, Higashiyama-ku, Kyoto

* Mushiki-ken tearoom: Ura Senke school of tea, Teranouchi, Ogawa-dori, Kamikyo-ku, Kyoto

* Omote Senke school of tea: Teranouchi, Ogawa-dori, Kamikyo-ku, Kyoto

Pavilion of Shimazu villa: Tamari, Kagoshima City, Kagoshima Prefecture

* Rinshun-kaku: Sankei-en, Hommoku-cho, Naka-ku, Yokohama

* Ryokaku-tei teahouse: Ninna-ji, Omuro Ouchi-cho, Ukyo-ku, Kyoto

* Ryu-tei pavilion: Koraku-en, Kokyo-cho, Okayama City, Okayama Prefecture

* Sa-an teahouse: abbot's residence, Gyokurin-in, Daitoku-ji, Daitokuji-cho, Murasakino, Kita-ku, Kyoto

Shinshin-an: Kusakawa-cho, Nanzenji, Sakyo-ku, Kyoto

Shisen-do: Ichijo-ji, Monguchi-cho, Sakyo-ku, Kyoto

Shoden Sanso villa: Kobata, Uji, Kyoto Prefecture

* Shogetsu-tei teahouse: abbot's residence, Sambo-in, Daigo-ji, Daigo Higashi-oji, Fushimi-ku, Kyoto

* Shoi-ken teahouse: Katsura villa, Katsura Misono-cho, Ukyo-ku, Kyoto

* Shokin-tei teahouse: Katsura villa, Katsura Misono-cho, Ukyo-ku, Kyoto

* Shonan-tei teahouse: Saiho-ji, Matsuo Kamigaya-cho, Ukyo-ku, Kyoto

* Shugaku-in imperial villa: Shugakuin, Sakyo-ku, Kyoto

Sochin-kyo pavilion: Shosei-en, Tamamizu-cho, Ainonachi-dori Shomen, Shimokyo-ku, Kyoto

Suzunoya: Matsuzaka Park, Matsuzaka, Mie Prefecture

Tai-an teahouse: Myoki-an, Oyamazaki, Otokuni-gun, Kyoto Prefecture

Tea hut: Inari Shrine, Yabunouchi-cho, Fushimi-ku, Kyoto

* Teigyoku-ken teahouse: abbot's residence, Shinju-an, Daitoku-ji, Daitokuji-cho, Murasakino, Kita-ku, Kyoto

Tennenzaku-tei pavilion: Tateda-cho, Otsu, Shiga Prefecture

Toin no Seki: Kita Hiyoshi-cho, Imakumano, Higashiyama-ku, Kyoto

* Ura Senke school of tea: Teranouchi, Ogawa-dori, Kamikyo-ku, Kyoto

* Zangetsu-tei: Omote Senke school of tea, Teranouchi, Ogawa-dori, Kamikyo-ku, Kyoto

Commentaries on the Photographs

6–7. FLOORING OF UNPAINTED WOOD. The natural beauty of the grain is enhanced by age and use.

10–11. MAIN GATE, KITAMURA RESIDENCE, KYOTO. The slender posts, the lightweight pantile roof, and the light-colored clay walls obviate any impression of heaviness. The fencelike construction in the foreground, with a gate of its own and its posts socketed in stones, has an ornamental rather than a protective function. At left, a tree in the garden wears the sheathing of straw that protects it in winter. At right, the tile-topped wall continues the pattern of the gate roof. The rectangular steppingstones in the background, leading from the gate to the main entrance, are placed in typical irregular order.

14–15. VIEW FROM INSIDE OF MAIN GATE, KITAMURA RESIDENCE. The steppingstones at center lead to the main entrance; the stone-paved walk at right, to the garden. Of particular interest here are the garden gate and fence, which are done in typically rustic style, combining wood, bamboo, and wooden shingles. The bench at left is a characteristic appurtenance of the sukiya style: a survival from the days when servants waited inside the gate while their masters visited the owners of the house.

16–17. MAIN ENTRANCE, KITAMURA RESIDENCE. The step is a large natural stone. At left are the shoji which serve as outer doors. Beyond the two-mat area are the fusuma or interior sliding doors. Again, as in the entrance gate, a bench (at right) is part of the structure. The two electric lights have been admirably adapted to the style of the house.

18, 19. OPEN CORRIDOR LEADING FROM GUEST ROOM TO TEAHOUSE, KITAMURA RESIDENCE. The dog-leg arrangement (page 18) is designed to add interest by providing a break in what would otherwise be an unrelieved straight passageway. The window at center on page 18 is the characteristic sukiya shitaji-mado: a lattice of bamboo laced with vine and backed with shoji. Typically slender posts of polished wood support the roof, and the board ceiling leaves the rafters exposed. The pavement is of ceramic tile. Also to be noted here is the stone gutter beyond the outer edge of the corridor. Its purpose is to supplement the gutter under the eaves during heavy rains and thereby to prevent mud puddles from forming in the garden.

20. MACHIAI (WAITING BOOTH) FOR TEA-CEREMONY GUESTS, KITAMURA RESIDENCE. Two benches, one of plain wood and the other covered with reed matting, are provided. Steppingstones are embedded in the earth floor. The machiai stands at the end of the corridor leading from the guest room to the teahouse. Here the guests wait until the host invites them to enter the teahouse itself.

21. STEPPINGSTONE PATH FROM GARDEN GATE TO OPEN CORRIDOR LEADING TO TEAHOUSE, KITAMURA RESIDENCE. The garden gate is in the background at right. The square stone basin was originally the pedestal for a Buddhist image. Mr. Kitamura found it abandoned on the premises of an old temple, bought it, and set it up in his garden, thus furnishing an excellent example of mitate—the discovery of new values in hitherto ignored objects.

22–23. POND AND TEAHOUSE VERANDA, KITAMURA RESIDENCE. Tea-ceremony guests enter the veranda on their way to the tearoom, stopping beside the stone basin for a ritual cleansing of their hands. The pond and rockwork are typical of traditional Japanese garden style. Of special interest here is the closing off of the upper part of the veranda with shoji to produce a more subdued light in the tearoom, which is located in the background at right.

24. TEAHOUSE VERANDA, KITAMURA RESIDENCE. The floor is composed of natural wood chosen for the beauty of its grain. Also to be noted is the distinguished design of the railing. The entrance to the tearoom is in the background at right.

25. Interior of tearoom, Kitamura residence. Although the photograph gives an impression of spaciousness, the tearoom has an area of only three tatami. The feeling of greater space is created by the slender posts, the largely undecorated wall areas, and the subtle lighting arrangements. The tokonoma, at rear, is in a style favored by the Edo-period tea master and designer Kobori Enshu. It is given an antique decorative touch by the pages from an old diary pasted at the bottom of its wall—another example of mitate.

26–27. Teahouse, Kitamura residence. Here the veranda, shown in detail on pages 22–23, is seen at right. The treatment of the roof, with its combination of shingles, thatch, and tile, and that of the posts, including one of bamboo and one retaining its bark, is highly individual and quite typical of the sukiya style. Although the rustic touch is plain to see, the handling of the details is decidedly sophisticated.

28, 29. Corridor between teahouse and shoin, Kitamura residence. The view on page 28 is toward the shoin; that on page 29, toward the teahouse. The elegance of the details hardly requires comment, but several features deserve special attention, among them the bamboo-lattice window (page 28, right), the ceiling of slender bamboo rods, and the polished boards of the natural-wood floor.

30–31. Veranda of shoin, Kitamura residence. The shoin is reached either by way of the corridor from the teahouse (pages 28, 29) or by means of a stepping-stone path through the garden. Although the eaves are quite broad, there is no need for more than two or three outer supporting posts, since the roof is comparatively light and beams and rafters bear much of the weight. The antique bronze lantern, like those seen elsewhere in the Kitamura residence, is typical of those found at temples and shrines. The stones in the background are not natural outcroppings but have been carefully selected and transported here to create the suggestion of a mountain landscape.

32. Detail of stonework at edge of shoin veranda, Kitamura residence. Persons entering the shoin by way of the garden path stop here to remove their footgear before stepping up onto the veranda. At top is the base of one of the supporting posts for the roof. Socketing such posts in stone gives the structure greater ability to withstand earthquakes.

33. Stone-paved passageway under eaves of shoin, Kitamura residence. When it is realized that the pavement here is composed of natural uncut stones, one can understand at least one of the reasons why the sukiya style is an expensive one. The large stone serves as a step. Here, once again, the great breadth of the eaves can be observed as well as the details of such supporting members as the posts and the beam extending between them.

34–35. Interior of shoin, Kitamura residence. Here the garden is viewed through the yukimi (snow-viewing) shoji, whose vertically sliding panels can be raised to uncover the glass panes at the bottom. The square board in the floor covers the pit in which charcoal is burned to boil water for tea or to heat the room in winter.

36. Bamboo blinds in shoin, Kitamura residence. In summer, shoji and glass doors are removed and replaced with blinds of split bamboo, which both shade the interior and allow the breeze to move freely through the room. The blinds may be raised or lowered as desired.

37. Corridor window of shoin, Kitamura residence. This arched window, cleanly cut into the clay wall, serves both to light the corridor and to frame a view of the garden.

38–39. Guest room of shoin, Kitamura residence. Here the quiet elegance of the sukiya style is epitomized in the clean lines of the component elements, the superb finish of the woodwork, and the neutral tones of the general décor. The scroll painting and the

flower arrangement in the tokonoma (right) are symbolic of winter. The plain fusuma (extreme left) and the unobtrusive pattern of the paper covering the sliding doors of the closet adjoining the tokonoma (left center) are in keeping with sukiya canons of decoration. At lower left is the square board covering the pit for the charcoal brazier.

42–43. Guest room of shoin in summer, Kitamura residence. The bamboo blinds that replace the shoji create an entirely new atmosphere in keeping with the season. In addition to subduing the intense outdoor light and allowing a maximum of ventilation, they assure a degree of privacy. Kyoto summers are oppressively hot, and even an illusion of coolness is welcome.

46–47. Aerial view of Rinshun-kaku, Sankei-en garden, Yokohama. The staggered arrangement of the buildings is an outstanding feature of the sukiya style. Besides allowing for the best use of outdoor light and for maximum ventilation, the arrangement provides for a wide variety of views, both interior and exterior, as well as interesting variations of roof styles. The roofing material here is wooden shingles.

51. Post and clay wall. Posts of this type were commonly used in feudal-period farmhouses. Their use in sukiya-style buildings is an example of mitate—the discovery of new values in commonplace objects and materials which ordinarily serve purely functional purposes and are otherwise ignored.

54–55. Jodan (raised-floor section) of Zangetsu-tei, Omote Senke school of tea, Kyoto. Originally designed for the seating of guests of high rank, this jodan now serves as a tokonoma. The hanging scroll is a portrait of Sen no Rikyu, tea master and originator of the sukiya style, and the room itself is a modified copy of his sixteenth-century Colored Shoin (see pages 182–83) at Juraku-dai. Both the jodan and the paulownia-crest pattern on the rear wall and the fusuma (left) are reminders that the military dictator Hideyoshi was a guest at the original Colored Shoin.

58–59. Aerial view of shoin buildings, garden, and lake, Katsura villa, Kyoto. A view like this one, though unnatural, is useful for showing the typical sukiya-style arrangement of the buildings, the various roof styles, and the diagonal lines of approach. Built in the seventeenth century, Katsura is the finest surviving example of early sukiya-style architecture.

62–63. Interior of Hasso no Seki, abbot's residence, Konchi-in, Nanzen-ji, Kyoto. This teahouse, designed by Kobori Enshu in the early seventeenth century, typifies his preference for well-lighted interiors. The placement of the windows is particularly interesting. At extreme right is the tokonoma; at lower left, the low sliding door by which guests enter the teahouse. The exposed framework of the ceiling (see detail on page 201), the clay walls pasted over with paper at the base, and the bamboo lattices at right—all these create an invitingly rustic atmosphere. The square section of tatami at lower right covers the pit for the charcoal brazier. Another detail of the teahouse appears on page 191.

66–67. Shonan-tei teahouse, Saiho-ji, Kyoto. This teahouse (see plan on pages 154–55) was built in the early seventeenth century by Sen no Rikyu's son Shoan as part of his retreat. It suggests a small mountain cottage of the type that served as the inspiration for the ceremonial teahouse, but even the most casual glance reveals the refinements of the sukiya style—for example, in the closely placed bamboo sections under the veranda, the ceiling above the veranda, and the slender supporting posts of the structure itself. A detail view of the Shonan-tei appears on pages 160–61.

70–71. Shitaji-mado (bamboo-lattice window), Konnichi-an tearoom, Ura Senke school of tea, Kyoto. This style of window, borrowed from the traditional minka or commoner's house and refined in typical sukiya fashion, is a trademark of the teahouse. The pattern created by the shadow of the bamboo lattice on the shoji has a special charm. The bottom of the clay wall is pasted over with sections from an old-time handwritten scroll.

74–75. Section of façade, Ichiriki-tei, Kyoto. The Ichiriki-tei is a celebrated restaurant dating from Edo times. In this detail view the pattern of the tilework over the eaves creates an interesting contrast with the patterns of the wooden lattice over the window beneath and the *inu-yarai* latticework which leans against the building. The literal meaning of inu-yarai is "dog barrier" (the function should be obvious), but its purpose today is more ornamental than purely functional, since wandering dogs are a good deal more rare than they were when the Ichiriki-tei was first built.

78–79. Reed-and-bamboo ceiling. Carefully selected marsh reeds are woven together and placed over rafters of bamboo to create a ceiling which emphasizes the natural beauty of the materials.

93. View of inner garden, Kasui-en, Miyako Hotel, Kyoto. Here the garden, with its islands of moss in a ground cover of carefully raked sand, is seen from one of the entrances. The harmony of straight-line composition is particularly well illustrated in this detail view of a modern structure in sukiya style.

96–97. Interior of Ko Shoin (Old Shoin), Katsura villa, Kyoto. As the finest surviving example of early sukiya architecture, the Katsura villa displays a purity of form that continues to inspire architects of the modern age. The "flexible interior" is well demonstrated here in the removable fusuma and the rather carefree placement of the posts. At left is the tokonoma, with its rustic-style post of polished wood. The light and airy-looking woodwork of the transom is a notable feature here. The paulownia-crest pattern of the paper on the tokonoma walls and the fusuma (see detail on page 177) signifies that the villa is now an imperial property.

100–101. Aerial view of central Kyoto. Although many of the buildings seen here are basically in minka style, they often employ details of the sukiya style in their construction. This section of the city is obviously quite crowded, and space for gardens is extremely limited. For this reason the garden usually takes the form of a small inner court. Traditionally the Kyoto building lot was long and narrow (about 50 by 100 feet), and the gables of houses were at the side rather than at front and rear—hence the general roof pattern observable in this photograph. Almost invariably the roofs are of tile because of the constant danger of fire. Many of these houses date from the seventeenth century.

104–5. Miyuki Room, Hassho-kan restaurant, Nagoya. The Hassho-kan, designed in the 1940's by Sutemi Horiguchi, is a superlative example of modern sukiya-style architecture. This room, whose name carries connotations of imperial visitors, serves for banquets as well as for tea-ceremony performances and flower-arrangement exhibits. The exquisiteness of its appointments scarcely requires comment, but the skylight and the patterns of the shoji and the lacquered tables are of special interest.

109. Steppingstones in a bed of moss. Natural stones, carefully placed to create a pleasing pattern of irregular shapes, often take the place of a paved or graveled walk as an approach to a sukiya-style building.

112–13. Aerial view of Katsura villa and garden, Kyoto. This view of the Katsura villa, although it is a totally abnormal one and probably could never have been imagined by the designers, has the virtue of showing the roof system of varying styles and materials (tile at top of photograph, shingles below) and the various diagonal-line approaches. Katsura's lake and garden are no less famous than the villa itself.

116. Approach to Fushin-an teahouse, Omote Senke school of tea, Kyoto. The steppingstones here furnish another example of the diagonal-line approach.

The teahouse itself suggests a rustic retreat far away from the hubbub of civilization, and the garden is meant to create an atmosphere of tranquility. The bamboo fence at right rear is especially worth noting. A detail of the Fushin-an appears on pages 152–53.

117. Steppingstones and stone steps leading to entrance of shoin buildings, Katsura villa, Kyoto. The ground cover is moss, which is also allowed to grow on the steps. More interesting, perhaps, is the clay wall with its topping of tile and its baseboard of weathered wood. The warm color of the clay is a typical sukiya characteristic.

118–19. Garden paths, Ura Senke school of tea, Kyoto. The gate at left, suspended from above, symbolizes the dividing line between the world of the teahouse and the world outside. The brushwood fence at center is a typical rustic touch. At right is the thatch-roofed Yu-in teahouse.

120–21. Approach to main entrance, Omote Senke school of tea, Kyoto. The stone-paved walk, bordered by beds of black river pebbles and screens of shrubbery clipped to resemble walls, curves to the left as it approaches the main entrance. Beyond the tile-topped clay wall is the garden. Like Ura Senke, Omote Senke is both a school of the tea ceremony and the residence of its master.

122. Approach to Ura Senke school of tea, Kyoto. In this example of the diagonal-line approach the walk is paved with natural stones set in cement. The trees and shrubbery along the path suggest a natural woodland setting.

123. Main entrance, Ura Senke school of tea, Kyoto. Wood, bamboo, clay, and tile are brought together in a composition that might almost be called a summary of sukiya materials, textures, and patterns. Of these, it is perhaps the patterns that command most attention here—for example, those of the bamboo fence and bamboo-surfaced step, the tile, the framework under the broad eaves, and the lower part of the shoji (woven strips of wood). At upper center is an old-fashioned gong. (See detail on page 125.)

124. Naka-kuguri (window-gate), Omote Senke school of tea, Kyoto. This quaint construction stands across the steppingstone path that leads into the tea garden (see plan on pages 126–27). Actually, it is a detached wall of clay with wooden posts and a window-like aperture through which the guests pass as they make a tour of the garden. Thus it may be said to symbolize the division between the everyday world outside and the tranquil world of the tea ceremony.

125. Detail of main entrance, Ura Senke school of tea, Kyoto. Here the quiet attractiveness of sukiya textures and patterns is revealed in greater detail than in the photograph on page 123. The design of the shoji is especially pleasing. The sections of woven wood strips at the bottom give an appropriately rustic air to the entrance, but there is nothing primitive about the workmanship. Here, too, the desired "patina of age" is quite evident.

129. Detail of tiled roof. When the sukiya style makes use of the tiled roof, it prefers the lightweight pantile known as sangawara to the older and heavier hongawara used on the roofs of temples and shrines. This detail of sangawara tiling reveals not only its pleasing pattern but also the effect of lightness it creates.

132–33. Ryokaku-tei teahouse, Ninna-ji, Kyoto. This teahouse, which is said to have been the property of the artist Ogata Korin (1658–1716), is quite large in comparison with the traditional teahouse from which the sukiya style originated. In fact, it is almost as large as the average dwelling house. (See plan on page 85.) Perhaps its most notable exterior feature is its light and graceful shingled roof. The stone lantern and water basin (extreme right) are characteristic adjuncts of the traditional tea garden. Detail photographs of the teahouse appear on pages 148 and 192–93.

134–35. Kami no Chaya (Upper Teahouse) and view of garden, Shugaku-in imperial villa, Kyoto. Shugaku-in, designed by the emperor Gomizuno-o and built for him in the seventeenth century, is not only an outstanding example of sukiya-style architecture but is also celebrated for its magnificent hillside setting. The Kami no Chaya is one of several buildings located at various places in the grounds of the villa. This view of it across the garden lake emphasizes an important principle of the sukiya style: the intimate relation of architecture to natural surroundings.

136–37. Detail of Shoi-ken teahouse, Katsura villa, Kyoto. Two notable features of the sukiya style are highlighted here: the bamboo-lattice window and the unorthodox pattern of the shoji grid. The bamboo-lattice window in this case takes two forms: the circular transoms above the shoji and the floor-level window in the clay wall at left. In both instances the apertures are backed by small shoji which can be opened to permit ventilation. Also of interest in this detail of the Shoi-ken is the harmony achieved within a complexity of geometric patterns. A full view of the teahouse appears on pages 138–39.

138–39. Shoi-ken teahouse, Katsura villa, Kyoto. This wintertime view of the Shoi-ken makes it appear no less inviting than in more clement seasons, when its interior can be opened to the outdoors. The warm color of its clay walls, the comfortable look of its thatched roof, and the general air of refined rusticity that it displays—all these suggest a pleasant retreat from the turmoil of the outside world. The shoji entrance (see detail on pages 136–37) is adjoined by a latticed window at right and is reached by a stone-paved walk. The large stones at the edge of the veranda (left of center) serve as steps.

140. Gable of Zangetsu-tei, Omote Senke school of tea, Kyoto. The shingled roof of the Zangetsu-tei is surmounted by a ridge cover consisting of shingles and an arrangement of bamboo poles designed to hold them in place. The understructure of the eaves also makes use of bamboo. The elements of design seen here are a reflection of the taste of Sen no Rikyu, whose Colored Shoin at Juraku-dai was copied in the Zangetsu-tei (photographs of interior on pages 54–55 and 182–83; plan on pages 174–75).

141. Detail of Shogetsu-tei teahouse, Sambo-in, Daigo-ji, Kyoto. Sambo-in, within the precincts of Daigo-ji temple, was one of the interests of the military dictator Toyotomi Hideyoshi (1536–98), who undertook its restoration after it had suffered from fire and neglect. The Shogetsu-tei (see also photograph on pages 186–87) is part of the abbot's residence and dates from Hideyoshi's time. At upper left, under the shoji window, is the low sliding door by which guests enter the tearoom after rinsing their hands at the stone basin. The dipper and the rods of bamboo that support it are laid across the basin in characteristic off-center style. Here once again, in the placement of rocks, building, and garden pond, the integration of architecture with nature is well illustrated.

142–43. Shokin-tei, teahouse, Katsura villa, Kyoto. The Shokin-tei is undoubtedly one of the most interesting of the buildings that comprise the Katsura villa. Its exterior appearance is quite simple and rustic, but its structural design and its interior arrangements are strikingly sophisticated. (See plan, pages 162–63, and detail photographs, pages 164–65, 184–85.) The entrance is at left, marked by two shoji doors. The six shoji to the right of the entrance are those of the 9-mat guest room. Behind the low screen at the center of the veranda is a small enclosure where water may be boiled for tea and simple cooking may be done (detail on pages 164–65). There is a similar arrangement on the rear veranda.

144–47. Kikugetsu-tei, Ritsurin Park, Takamatsu, Kagawa Prefecture. Although daimyo and samurai were required to maintain official residences whose structure and decoration reflected their social status, they could build private villas in which no status symbols were necessary at all. For such construction they almost invariably employed the sukiya style, and the building seen here is a superb expression of that style. The Kikugetsu-tei and the adjoining Sho-en-kan (see plan on pages 88–89) were built in the late seventeenth century for Matsudaira Yorishige, lord of Sanuki Province (now Kagawa Prefecture) in Shikoku, and are preserved today in a public park. The diagonal-line arrangement of the component buildings, the broad verandas, the slender posts, the lightweight shingled roofs, the general openness of the construction—all these lend the villa an air of gracefulness that makes it a major attraction among surviving examples of sukiya-style architecture in the feudal period.

148. Detail of veranda, Ryokaku-tei teahouse, Ninna-ji, Kyoto. Here the clay used for the walls has been mixed with straw both to strengthen it and to enhance the rustic effect, which is essentially that of a farmhouse. The same effect is achieved in the tokonoma (pages 192–93). Bamboo is used for the framework of the eaves, the lattices of the windows, the floor of the veranda, and the corner post seen at right of center. The Ryokaku-tei, now some three centuries old, may well reflect the taste of the celebrated Edo-period artist Ogata Korin, to whom it reputedly belonged, for Korin was, above all, a master of design. The building itself appears on pages 132–33; its plan, on page 85.

149. Detail of abbot's residence, Sambo-in, Daigo-ji, Kyoto. Part of the veranda of the shoin room is seen across an inner-court garden. The base of the post in the foreground has been carefully cut to fit the contours of the natural stone on which it rests. This construction technique, in addition to assuring greater stability against earthquakes, furnishes a rustic touch that is particularly valued by the sukiya style, although it is used in other traditional styles of Japanese architecture as well.

152–53. Detail of Fushin-an teahouse, Omote Senke school of tea, Kyoto. At extreme right is the nijiri-guchi, the low sliding-door aperture by which guests enter the tearoom. The usual explanation of this traditional entrance is that the guests, by assuming a humble posture to go through it, put themselves in a proper mood for the tea ceremony. In a word, pride and vanity and worldly concerns are left behind. This may be true, but it appears that the nijiri-guchi was originally created for another psychological purpose—that is, to make the small tearoom seem larger once the guests had entered it through an abnormally small door. Here, once again, the shitaji-mado (bamboo-lattice window) and the clay wall display the attractions that first inspired the tea masters to adapt them from the minka style. The photograph on page 116 shows the Fushin-an teahouse itself and the steppingstone approach to the nijiri-guchi.

157. Detail of bamboo-floored veranda. It is quite obvious here that the bamboo has been selected with extreme care, not only to insure uniformity of size and smoothness of placement but also to produce a pleasing pattern. Bamboo, like wood, must be properly aged before it can be used for construction purposes.

160–61. Detail of Shonan-tei teahouse, Saiho-ji, Kyoto. The veranda (see photograph on pages 66–67) is at the left. The stone at left of center in the lower half of the photograph serves as a step. The shoji at center, with their bottom sections of wood, represent an interesting variation of a traditional form. Another variation is seen in the shoji of the window at right. The plan of the Shonan-tei appears on pages 154–55.

164–65. Veranda, Shokin-tei teahouse, Katsura villa, Kyoto. In the foreground is an enclosure with a fireplace where water is boiled for tea and simple cooking can be done. At right is a portion of the 9-mat guest room. Features of particular interest here include the natural logs used for the two corner posts and the beam at left, the bamboo-and-reed ceiling above the veranda, and the brushwood screen underneath. Beyond the swinging door of woven cryptomeria strips at center is the entrance to the teahouse. Other photographs of the Shokin-tei appear on pages 142–43 and 184–85; its plan, on pages 162–63.

166–67. MOON-VIEWING VERANDA OF MAIN SHOIN BUILDING, KATSURA VILLA, KYOTO. This open veranda of bamboo is an extension of the wood-floored veranda in the foreground. Actually it is a *dai* or platform, and the literal translation of its Japanese name, *tsukimi-dai*, is "moon-viewing platform." There is an appealing contrast here between the texture and pattern of wood and bamboo. Both materials have taken on the "patina of age" prized by sukiya designers. It should be noted that the blue of the wooden floor and the shoji at right is not their actual color but is, instead, an effect occasioned by the lighting of the photograph.

168–69. DETAIL OF KOHO-AN, ABBOT'S RESIDENCE, DAITOKU-JI, KYOTO. At center and right is the veranda, partially enclosed by shoji and overlooking the garden. The room in the left foreground is the famous Bosen tearoom, originally designed by Kobori Enshu. The larger room beyond it serves for the reception of guests. The wooden sliding doors at center open on a corridor.

170–71. RYU-TEI PAVILION, KORAKU-EN, OKAYAMA CITY. This structure was originally intended for the holding of poetry parties. Guests sat on the two verandas, facing the small stream that flows among the rocks at right of center. The first part of a poem would be composed by those sitting at the far end of either veranda and floated downstream in a sakè cup while guests at the near end composed the latter half. The features of chief interest here, in addition to the light and airy structure itself, are the slender posts, the polished wooden floors, and the incorporation of nature into the very heart of the building.

172. DETAIL OF VERANDA, BLACK SHOIN, NISHI HONGAN-JI, KYOTO. The floor in the foreground is composed of unusually broad planks of polished wood; the small section in the background at right is of bamboo. At upper left is a natural-stone basin into which a depression has been carved to hold water. The bamboo wall at top is of particularly pleasing design.

173. DETAIL OF TEIGYOKU-KEN TEAHOUSE, SHINJU-AN, DAITOKU-JI, KYOTO. Here an earth-floored recess with a bamboo-lattice window and a removable bamboo partition open at the bottom contains the stone water basin (lower left) at which tea-ceremony guests rinse their hands. The rack at upper right served in olden times as a place for samurai to leave their swords before entering the tearoom, since it was unthinkable that one should have a weapon with him during the tea ritual. When the tea ceremony is held at night, a lantern is placed on the flat-topped stone at lower right.

177. FUSUMA WITH PAULOWNIA-CREST PATTERN, KO SHOIN, KATSURA VILLA, KYOTO. The stylized paulownia design seen here—three leaves with three spikes of five, seven, and five flowers respectively—is one of the crests of the imperial family, and its use at Katsura signifies that the villa is now an imperial property. Hideyoshi's paulownia crest, seen in the Zangetsu-tei (pages 54–55), is a variant of this one, with spikes of three, five, and three flowers.

180–81. INTERIOR OF KYUSUI-KEN PAVILION, SHU-GAKU-IN IMPERIAL VILLA, KYOTO. The Shugaku-in villa, built in the seventeenth century for the emperor Gomizuno-o, was designed by the emperor himself. The fastidious taste displayed in the Kyusui-ken makes it one of the finest monuments of the early sukiya style. At left is the broad-silled shoin-style window. The raised-floor areas served for the seating of the emperor and guests of imperial rank. Most remarkable here is the elegant simplicity of the design and the complete absence of extraneous decoration.

182–83. INTERIOR OF ZANGETSU-TEI, OMOTE SENKE SCHOOL OF TEA, KYOTO. In this view the jodan (raised-floor area), seen in detail on pages 54–55, appears at left. At right rear is the shoin window with its broad sill. The two types of ceiling visible here—broad boards above the jodan, narrow boards and exposed bamboo rafters at right—illustrate the predilection of the sukiya style for variety and individuality of presentation. A small old-fashioned temple bell hangs

above the shoin window. As a prototype of sukiya-style architecture, the Zangetsu-tei represents an interesting summary of its characteristic features. (See plan on pages 174–75.)

184–85. INTERIOR OF GUEST ROOM, SHOKIN-TEI TEAHOUSE, KATSURA VILLA, KYOTO. The Shokin-tei teahouse (see other views on pages 142–43 and 164–65, plan on pages 162–63) is somewhat more bold in its interior décor than most other sukiya-style buildings pictured in this book. The fusuma, for example, display a rather prominent pattern, and the ink paintings on the sliding doors of the closet at top right draw considerable attention to themselves. Nevertheless, the rules of sukiya taste are not violated. At right rear, adjoined by sliding-door closets and only partly visible, is the tokonoma, whose walls repeat the pattern of the fusuma. The veranda is at extreme left.

186–87. CIRCULAR WINDOW, SHOGETSU-TEI TEA-HOUSE, SAMBO-IN, DAIGO-JI, KYOTO. The perfectly round window is uncommon in traditional Japanese architecture, but here it symbolizes the individuality of the sukiya style. Its shoji, of course, are rectangular, and the combination of straight and curved lines in this case has considerable charm. At left is the characteristic teahouse window with a bamboo lattice. Another detail of the Shogetsu-tei appears on page 141.

188–89. YUKIMI (SNOW-VIEWING) SHOJI AND BAMBOO-FLOORED VERANDA, HASSHO-KAN RESTAURANT, NAGOYA. Here the vertically sliding panels of the shoji have been raised to give a view of the garden through the glass sections at the bottom. The bamboo moon-viewing platform is also seen. The Hassho-kan is one of the most outstanding modern structures in sukiya style. Its Miyuki Room appears on pages 104–5.

190. TOKONOMA, KAN'IN TEAROOM, ABBOT'S RESIDENCE, JUKO-IN, KYOTO. The rustic charm of this tokonoma is plain to see, not only in its clay wall and its framework (the main post is at right) but also in the small and unpretentious window at its left side. The calligraphic scroll bears a Zen motto urging renunciation of egotistic and worldly thoughts and concentration on the sublime. The typical tea-ceremony flower arrangement consists of a single white camellia and its foliage in a hanging container of rough pottery. Since the usual tea garden has no flowers, a simple arrangement like this one is designed to furnish the guests with a refreshing surprise and at the same time to express the essence of floral beauty.

191. DETAIL OF HASSO NO SEKI, ABBOT'S RESIDENCE, KONCHI-IN, NANZEN-JI, KYOTO. This strikingly individual teahouse (see other views on pages 62–63 and 201) was designed by Kobori Enshu in the seventeenth century. In many ways it is the epitome of the Enshu style, which is characterized chiefly by its light and comparatively open construction. This detail shows the arched sliding door by which the host enters the tearoom, the extended wall—part clay, part bamboo lattice—adjoining the tokonoma, and the clay walls papered over at the base. The post at center retains the natural curve of the tree from which it was cut.

192–93. TOKONOMA (RIGHT) AND ADJOINING SHELVES AND CLOSET, RYOKAKU-TEI TEAHOUSE, NINNA-JI, KYOTO. The same mixture of clay and straw noted in the earlier detail of this teahouse (page 148) is used here for the walls, and its extremely rustic effect is echoed in the tokonoma post at center. Here, perhaps more than anywhere else in this teahouse, the individuality of the style suggests that the original designer-owner may indeed have been the artist Ogata Korin, whose striking sense of design is best exemplified in his celebrated decorative screens. The teahouse itself appears on pages 132–33; its plan, on page 85.

194. DETAIL OF MUSHIKI-KEN TEAROOM, URA SENKE SCHOOL OF TEA, KYOTO. Unusually broad fusuma form one partition of the room and reflect the outdoor light from the window at right. The uncovered section of board flooring at lower right is a characteristic variation of the sukiya tearoom style. Adjoining it is the pit for the charcoal brazier, here shown uncovered. The

lattice, laced with vines, and the adze-cut post supply the proper rustic touch to this quietly elegant interior.

195. SHOJI IN SHOIN, KATSURA VILLA, KYOTO. The utter simplicity displayed here might almost be said to represent an idealization of the shoji. All decoration is rejected; there are no bottom panels of wood or glass —nothing but the pleasing pattern of the grid and the warm translucence of the paper. The shoji of the transom admit less light because of the broad eaves, but on a bright day the shadow of the lattice just outside them combines with their grid to make another attractive design.

196. DETAIL OF TATAMI FLOOR. The attractions of the tatami are numerous: the inviting texture of the reed surface, the warm yellowish color (or pale green when the tatami are quite new), the pattern created by the weave and the tape binding of the edges, the resilience provided by the thick mat of woven straw underneath. In this detail photograph three tatami come together in a typical asymmetric arrangement.

197. TEAROOM CHARCOAL PIT. The lacquered frame is decorated with paulownia and chrysanthemum crests, and the tatami is especially woven to accommodate the pit. The three iron prongs serve to support the kettle in which water is boiled for making ceremonial tea. Two types of charcoal are seen here: the black cylindrical type cut from the thicker branches of trees and the white type made from twigs. Both are quite special and, like the bed of white ashes underneath, have been selected with great care to express the aesthetic consciousness of the host at the tea ceremony.

198. REED SHOJI (TOP) AND REED BLINDS (BOTTOM). These summertime accessories are designed not only to aid ventilation but also (and more importantly) to control the lighting within a room. The reeds, like those often used for ceilings, are chosen with special care and are woven so that their joints create a pattern. Split bamboo is not used for shoji of this type, although it is frequently used for blinds (pages 42–43). The intention here, once again, is to produce the rustic effect that is typical of the sukiya style.

199. DETAIL OF YUKIMI (SNOW-VIEWING) SHOJI AND INNER GARDEN, KITCHO RESTAURANT, OSAKA. The vertically sliding panels of the yukimi shoji have been raised to uncover the bottom sections of glass and to allow a partial view of a tiny inner-court garden. Essentially the shoji serve here as a frame for a small picture, at the same time bringing a bit of nature inside. In doing this, they enhance the beauty of the garden itself by highlighting such details as the ferns, the moss, the lichened tree trunk, and the antique stone lantern. This limited view, in a word, is more intriguing than a full view of the garden would be.

200. CEILING, GEPPA-RO PAVILION, KATSURA VILLA, KYOTO. The Japanese name for this style of ceiling is

kesho yaneura—literally, "decorative garret," although in fact the "garret" has no floor. Bamboo, reed, and wood (see detail photograph on page 204)—all carefully selected for texture and durability—are assembled in an ostensibly rustic but nonetheless sophisticated pattern. The suggestion of a farmhouse is quite plain, but the treatment, in typical sukiya fashion, is anything but primitive. The tablet hanging below the ceiling bears the characters for "moon" (left) and "poetry" or "song" (right), signifying that the Geppa-ro (literally, "Moon Wave Pavilion") was designed as a pleasant retreat for the owners of the Katsura villa as well as for their guests.

201. DETAIL OF CEILING, HASSO NO SEKI, ABBOT'S RESIDENCE, KONCHI-IN, NANZEN-JI, KYOTO. In this detail photograph of the Hasso no Seki (see other views on pages 62–63 and 191) the ceiling is viewed from outside the arched doorway by which the tea-ceremony host enters. Two styles of ceiling construction are seen here: unpainted boards laid over a framework of bamboo tied with twine (center) and reed matting supported by slender bamboo poles (left). The deliberately rustic air of the teahouse is enhanced not only by the ceiling but also by the roughly finished clay walls and the adze-cut posts and beams. The Hasso so Seki, now well over three centuries old, is a monument to the taste of the tea master Kobori Enshu, who designed it in the early seventeenth century.

202-3. DETAIL OF INTERIOR, SA-AN TEAHOUSE, ABBOT'S RESIDENCE, GYOKURIN-IN, DAITOKU-JI, KYOTO. Although the Sa-an is furnished with a skylight and several windows, the lighting is deliberately subdued in keeping with the most orthodox tea-ceremony traditions. The dark-toned walls, in which straw has been mixed with the clay to give it greater strength, absorb rather than reflect the limited light. The atmosphere may at first glance appear to be somber, but actually it is quite warm and inviting. The windows seen here are of the characteristic bamboo-lattice type, the one at the right being provided with an adjoining frame into which the shoji slides when it is opened. The slender bamboo post just left of center forms a part of this frame but does not function as a support for the beam above. In front of the window at extreme left is a hanging shelf.

204. DETAIL OF CEILING, GEPPA-RO PAVILION, KATSURA VILLA, KYOTO. Here the details of construction can be more clearly observed than in the view of the ceiling on page 200, and the pattern created by the materials —bamboo, wood, and reed—becomes more plain. The ridge beam rests on a post of unfinished wood in natural form. The bamboo rafters are supplemented at strategic points by rafters of wood. Although the design of the ceiling is considerably more intricate than that of most other sukiya-style ceilings pictured in this book, it does not convey an impression of heaviness.

Glossary-Index

NOTE: Numbers in italics indicate pages on which illustrations appear.

The "weathermark" identifies this English-language edition as having been planned and produced at the editorial offices of John Weatherhill, Inc., 7-6-13 Roppongi, Minato-ku, Tokyo, based upon the Japanese edition of Tankosha, Kyoto. Architectural drawings by Mitsuru Suzuki, Shunsuke Itoh, and Hironari Kanno. Composition and letterpress printing by Kenkyusha, Tokyo. Plates engraved and printed by Nissha, Kyoto. Bound at the Makoto Binderies, Tokyo. Text set in Monotype Garamond, with handset Optima for display.